The Story of
Crofting
in Scotland

Other books by Douglas Willis

Discovering the Black Isle
A Scottish Nature Diary

The Story of Crofting in Scotland

DOUGLAS WILLIS

JOHN DONALD PUBLISHERS LTD
EDINBURGH

John Donald Publishers Ltd.,
138 St Stephen Street, Edinburgh EH3 5AA.

ISBN 0 85976 344 7

British Library Cataloguing-in-Publication Data.

A catalogue record for this book is available from
the British Library.

Typeset by Pioneer Associates, Perthshire
Printed & bound in Great Britain by
Arrowsmith Ltd., Bristol

Contents

Location map of crofting areas.

Introduction

The crofting landscape of the Highlands and Islands of Scotland is without doubt one of the most distinctive in all of western Europe. Central to this distinctiveness are the ordered small landholdings, the townships with their lines and scatters of croft houses, and the common grazings.

There are two ways in which crofting may be said to represent a living 'at the edge'. Firstly, in its geographical setting, it is very much a feature of Europe's most peripheral part – the continent's Atlantic edge. Secondly, in an economic sense, it represents a living often characterised by a position on the edge of viability. Marginality has always been a hallmark of crofting agriculture, and life could not be sustained in the crofting areas without recourse to an almost endless list of supplementary occupations.

In an age that romanticises the ideal of a small country living, there is sometimes a popular perception of crofting that conjures up an image of the 'good life' where the croft, in exchange for some measure of human input, will obligingly supply a satisfying family living. In fact, nothing could be further removed from the truth. Those who have aspired towards the good life via crofting have often been doomed to disappointment.

Crofting exists in a setting that may be beautiful and even spectacular to look at, but it is impossible to feed a family off the scenery, and there is an inherent challenge in living there. To a

1

large extent crofting has its existence in the same peripheral setting which supported settlement in the earliest peopling of the area many centuries ago. Yet crofting itself is nothing ancient. In fact, in terms of Highland history, it is decidedly modern.

Crofting also presents an enigmatic front to those who look upon its outward face with no knowledge of its past. Why, for example, do many crofts crowd together in such unrewarding places at the very edge of the land, when more fertile-looking inland valleys not many miles away are empty of people? And why are those same straths marked by the crumbling ruins that are such a poignant presence amid the emptiness?

The answer must be sought in the origins of crofting; in the conscious desire of landowners in the early part of the last century to reshape the land-use pattern of their estates. But first it was necessary to redistribute the farming folk who peopled them. The changes that were wrought in this transformation were dramatic, to say the least. The enforced shift away from an economy that aspired towards farming self-sufficiency to a hybrid form of living based on both the land and the maritime resources which fringed it, involved a whole people who had little power to resist. The land which their ancestors had worked may have seemed theirs by right, but it was not theirs by law.

Such mass manipulation of a people could scarcely have been achieved without its problems. The words 'clearance', 'eviction' and 'emigration' liberally lace the crofters' story in the popular mind, as though theirs was a lost cause, the people mere pawns in a situation which they were unable to influence. In fact, although this shift to form the crofting settlements involved one of the great forced population movements of European history, there was a spirit of resistance among the people that was to find a later flowering in the Crofters' War of the second half of the last century. Indeed, this pattern of events so alarmed the government that it was obliged to embark on a policy of gunboat diplomacy round its very own shores. Civil disobedience may be regarded as a phenomenon of our age, but the crofters of last century were well practised in its art, and not afraid to stand up to the power of the law in defence of their cause. The etchings of township scenes of the crofter women taking on the full might of the military must indeed have amazed the gentlemen

Crofts on the isolated Shetland island of Fair Isle.

in their comfortable southern clubs as they pored over the pages of the *Illustrated London News* and the like.

So impressive did this show of power become that the government was forced to take the extreme step of setting up a Royal Commission to enquire into the crofters' circumstances. The Napier Commission Report published in 1884 brought the aggrieved voice of crofters to the nation's attention. This milestone in crofting matters was followed in turn by the Crofters Act of 1886 which laid down the first statutory guidelines for the organisation of crofting, safeguarding the rights of the individual crofters and giving to them the security that would be an incentive to improve their land. Successive governments have added substantially to the code of crofting law. Today, there is still a Crofters Commission charged with overseeing the practice of crofting, and nowhere else in the land does there exist any comparable group of people with their way of life bound by such a special code of legislation.

Though monetary wealth might be an unattainable dream for the crofting generations, they nevertheless had a richness of culture that found its expression in the Gaelic language and in the Northern Isles' tongue with its legacy of Old Norn. It was richly expressed, too, in customs and material culture. The buildings in which the people lived and worked expressed an intimate link with the land in which they were set and out of which they were fashioned. The houses and their interior plenishings may have represented merely the basic requirements for living, but they hold much interest for us today in an age which eschews vernacular style and offers little place for the traditional and the home-made.

Ironically, perhaps, in an age of improved communication, much of the crofting province is at a greater economic disadvantage because of its geographical location than ever before. Livestock producers throughout the crofting area are challenged to compete with farmers in far more favoured locations, and traditionally they have had to be content with the role of producers of store animals which those more advantaged areas could profitably finish off for market. Communications are the key to survival for remoter communities, and a widespread programme of ferry, bridge, causeway and road improvement in recent times has been giving crofters better links than their predecessors had.

Perhaps not since the days of unrest has crofting enjoyed the high profile which surrounds it at the present time. Demand for vacant crofts is considerable in areas where, two or three decades ago, there was no interest at all and rural depopulation was rife. There is an encouraging enthusiasm among younger members of the crofting community in many areas, and crofting has been viewed in some quarters as a model for the kind of countryside economy that the government would wish to encourage, namely one where a complete rural dependence on agriculture is reduced. In the last few years, the Crofters' Union has also given crofting matters a much higher profile. Nor has the wider political dimension in crofting gone away. Early in 1991, the Labour Party promised a crofting review.

In no way is this book intended as an in-depth analysis of the crofting community. Other writers have most effectively done that job already. Rather it is an attempt, at a time when interest in the subject is strong, to present the more general story of crofting in Scotland, from past through to present.

CHAPTER 1

Landscape with crofts

The crofting scene is not so much a landscape of crofts as a landscape *with* crofts, for throughout the Highlands and Islands it is the land which dominates, and the crofts which often seem to fit in where they can. Nature has been niggardly with her favours in these peripheral parts of the realm, forcing the folk to adjust their ways to the challenge of living in a homeland of limited opportunity.

A glance at a map of the crofting area will confirm that it corresponds with one of the most difficult landscapes for human settlement in the whole of western Europe. Here is a land of constant contrast; a place where islands alternate with peninsulas; where these rugged fingers of land reach out into the Atlantic, and where fjord-like sea lochs indent deeply the fretted rim of the mainland's edge.

The west coast and the Western and Northern Isles thus lie at the outermost edge of the continent – what Professor Estyn Evans meaningfully called the 'Atlantic ends' of Europe. This landscape with crofts is therefore a landscape that is both limiting and challenging in the nature of its geography. If we are to appreciate the appearance of the crofting scene and understand something of its making, we must be aware of this environmental backcloth.

While a detailed knowledge of the complexities of Highland geology is hardly necessary for an understanding of crofting, the nature of the rocks has been such an important shaping influence on the land – and by extension on the people who have taken a living from it – that its characteristics and influences require to be borne in mind.

As in any area, the rocks which lie beneath impart much character to the surface scene above. The geological foundations of the crofting areas are something of a mixed bag. Some are impressively volcanic – the eroded relics of lava outpourings from deep down in the crust. These ancient earth offerings have had a profound influence on the scenery of the small isles

5

of the Inner Hebrides where Norse-named peaks rise above the lowland fringe of Rum and where the lofty Sgurr of Eigg oversees the comings and goings of the island scene around. But it is on the Isle of Skye that the volcanic legacy finds its most dramatic expression. Indeed, in some parts of the island an almost lunar landscape of rugged remains is suggested in the uprearing rock faces, the visual effect being at its most impressive when swirls of mist trail over the hills.

North of Iona and west of Mull lies a scatter of volcanic remains, including the Treshnish Isles and Staffa with Fingal's cave, a feature so dramatic that it provided the inspiration for the composer Mendelssohn in penning his 'Hebridean Overture'. Where the extrusions from below started to lose their fierce heat before reaching the surface, the process of slow cooling created the crystal-rich granites of the Ross of Mull and of the rocky peninsula of Ardnamurchan, most westerly extension of the entire Scottish mainland.

It can be said, therefore, that crofting has its setting in an antique land, for other of the Highland rocks are more ancient still. The Lewisian gneiss, which so dominates the crofting landscape of Lewis and Harris and parts of the western mainland, is one of the most ancient of all European rocks. Super-heated and completely altered in form, the gneiss has known geological change on the grandest of scales. Ground down through the aeons of time by the ongoing powers of erosion, this hard grey foundation is the basis of a low-lying landscape that is pitted with a multitude of depressions now filled with larger lochs and peaty dubh lochans which hold the abundant rainfall and lend a distinctiveness to map and landscape. Indeed, the district to the south of Stornoway in Lewis where water almost dominates the whole landscape is appropriately known as Lochs.

In comparison, the dull red Torridonian sandstone is not quite as venerable, but when millions of years are being discussed, such differences are purely academic. What is important is that it dominates the rugged landscapes of Wester Ross and west Sutherland with their distinctive upland scenery, including such massifs as the characterful Quinag and Canisp, Cul Beag and Ben More Coigach, Suilven and Stac Pollaidh. These are real picture-postcard peaks, rising steeply and

Almost hidden among the ice-scoured rocks, crofts cling to whatever scraps of useful land they can on Harris's east side.

dramatically above the low-lying platform of the Lewisian gneiss below. Like benign, unchanging giants, they dwarf the coastal crofts. The red Torridonian rock was once much used in the building of croft houses and still distinguishes the older buildings in settlements like the Wester Ross village of Ullapool. The north-west mainland culminates in these ancient rock foundations at the wild and remote promontory of Cape Wrath.

These physical foundations of the crofting landscape are therefore as ancient as any in the land. Following them in the time sequence comes the Durness limestone whose outcropping is limited in its distribution, but whose presence is marked in the greener, sweeter grazings of the north-west mainland around the inland crofting districts of Elphin and Knockan, as well as in the scenic attractions of the caves of Assynt and at Smoo at Durness itself. The limestone leaves its own mark on the scenery, and in economic terms, the availability of a workable deposit has been responsible for the removal of millions of tons of rock from the quarry above Ullapool to provide agricultural lime to help neutralise the dour, acid soils of the west.

The grey moine schist is yet another dominating rock type over much of the west Highlands. It is easily recognisable by the fact that it sparkles in the sun, an effect created by its high mica content. It splits into the large, smooth sections sometimes seen at modern road improvements where blasting has revealed fresh rock faces. Where the rock has split into smaller slabs, its importance may be seen not only in the enduring stone dykes and sheep fanks erected by crofters in the past, but also in the walls of croft houses and in byres where it had such diverse uses as door and window lintels and livestock stall divisions.

In the more north-easterly province of the Highlands, from the firthlands of Easter Ross, up through the coastal fringe of Sutherland, into the low-lying plain of Caithness and over the Pentland Firth to Orkney, the rocks are of much younger, sedimentary formations. Unlike its hard and more aged red counterpart of the west, the old red sandstone is a softer rock by far. Where it occurs it has given a more fertile basis for land working, but it is the facility of the flagstone variant of the rock to split into comparatively thin layers that has been of value in this more northerly and Nordic crofting province where massive flagstones still delimit boundaries.

In Orkney, the sandstones have weathered to give a more rewarding kind of soil across the scatter of low green isles where farming, rather than crofting, tends to dominate the scene, but where crofts still make a significant contribution to the islands' land-use pattern. Only Hoy and Rousay deviate much from Orkney's low-lying character. The former, with its towering cliffs and Old Man of Hoy sea stack, is an upland place with its high Ward Hill dominating the once populous crofting township of Rackwick below.

Rousay recalls the moorland hills of mainland Scotland with its sandstone strata outcropping along the hill slopes. There is somehow a more Highland feel about parts of Rousay, an impression reinforced by the recollection of its crofting evictions, and which sets it apart from such green farming islands as Shapinsay and Stronsay to its south and east.

The small Shetland crofting outlier of Fair Isle lies as if cast adrift, equidistant from the two groups of northern isles. It continues the sandstone theme, as does the southern part of Mainland in Shetland, but towards the 'Ultima Thule' of north

Ruins of a croft at Corrie near Ullapool. Slabs of Moine schist rock have been used for lintels and byre stall divisions.

Mainland, Yell and Unst, the open *scattalds* or common grazings spread over rocks that are sometimes more reminiscent of those of the west Highlands, though there are significant differences. The uncommon steatite or soapstone of Unst provided the Norse forebears of the present crofters with a workable medium in which they could carve cooking pots more hard wearing by far than those produced from the coarse local clay.

The landscape of crofting is therefore strongly influenced in its character by the kind of rocks which underlie it. But there have been other influences, too; influences that have moulded and modified the lie of the land in dramatic ways. Foremost amongst these are the far-reaching effects of the Ice Age, when glaciers flowed seawards from snow-gathering hollows on the high hills. Studded with sharp rock scree, the ice made its slow seawards progress, widening and deepening its valley paths as it went, so that their present forms are a legacy of much colder times than now.

These wide and flat-bottomed U-shaped valleys are a dominant theme of so much of the geography of the Highlands, restricting human opportunity by the steepness of their sides, but providing a basis for land use and settlement along the flanks of their flat floors. They are commonly described as straths, and any map of the area shows how often the term prefixes the name of a river, like Strath Naver or Strath Conon. The names of some of these valleys are perhaps known more for their history than for their formation, for they are synonymous with the clearance of the folk who peopled them early last century.

The mountains of the Highlands come so close to the western edge that the erosive power of the glaciers was all the more concentrated. The result is seen not only in the ice-widened straths but in the deep sea lochs which closely resemble the Norwegian fjords in their form and in the manner of their making. When rising temperatures thawed the ice, and sent torrents of meltwater rushing off the land, the effect was to increase sea levels and inundate the seaward ends of glaciated valleys. In this way, the multitude of west coast sea lochs came into being as deep water reminders of this ancient process of landscape drowning.

For long, these western sea lochs were viewed in negative terms as a disruption to the line of north-south communication, making it easier for crofting communities to keep in touch by small boat rather than by road. But in more recent times their worth in terms of scenic value, and of recreation and fish farming potential, has been increasingly recognised.

When the great weight of glacial ice overlay the northern part of Scotland, it had a depressing effect on the land, causing it to sink. When the ice burden was removed with rising temperatures, the land began to recover once more. Stages in its recovery are marked by the raised beaches which so dominate the seaward edge along much of the west coast, and which have had an influence on the physical form of crofting settlements in many places.

Peat stack at Ness, Lewis. Peat continues to fulfil an important role as a fuel supply for crofting communities.

In terms of scenic appreciation, such tourist-frequented spots as Gruinard Bay in Wester Ross, with its classic sequence of raised beaches, are much admired by a steady stream of summer visitors. But few give a thought for those who have had to make a living in such circumstances — the ancestors of the folk who live along this Atlantic edge, and of today's crofters. In a land so dominated by steepness of slope and roughness of terrain, the flat fringe of land that is the raised beach was bound to be a positive feature in a landscape otherwise so negative in its character. In this regard, the crofting townships which trace the edges of the western sea lochs and line the northern voes have more than a passing resemblance to the beads of settlement one sees strung out along the edges of Norwegian fjords. There, the flat fringe of the *strandflat* provides a striking parallel to the Scottish raised beach. Indeed, the comparison confirms the similar response made by folk in different places to a similar set of circumstances.

But so much for the landscape's ancient legacy. Some of the

processes that have shaped the crofting scene are much less ancient than those of the chilly days of the Ice Age. Peat, now forming such an extensive covering blanket over the ancient rocks, is a product of no great antiquity. Its formation has been a feature of the post-glacial period, for at the end of the Ice Age the landscape slate had been wiped clean, as it were, by the erosive passage of the ice which scoured and scraped all that lay in its path. Highland rocks are invariably impervious to water, so that high rainfall and impeded drainage have together encouraged the widespread growth of bogs where *sphagnum* moss is the dominant plant species. In the waterlogged and airless bog conditions, the processes of decomposition of plant remains are reduced, and the result is a slow build-up of peat. Limited in their potential for land use, peatlands have nevertheless been a vitally important resource for the crofting areas, for cut peat has long provided a widely available, low-cost fuel supply. Places without access to peat banks were hard pressed in the old days, and in some of the Northern Isles where peat was completely absent, dried tangles and cow dung were commonly-used substitutes. Though peat has to compete now with imported fuels, it retains its traditional importance in many places, the blue reek of peat fires pervading the air throughout much of the crofting province.

By contrast to the peat bogs with their squelching sphagnum carpets, the *machair* — that western rim of sand-dominated landscape that fringes the Outer Hebrides and so dominates the inner Hebridean isle of Tiree — provides a dry and freely draining element. In origin it owes much to the prevailing westerly wind which has lifted the sand from the shore and deposited it over the land. The machair has become a dominating theme in the crofting life and landscape of island places such as the Uists, Benbecula, Barra and Tiree. It imparts a softer character to parts of the western edge of Lewis and more especially to south Harris where its mellowness stands in marked contrast to the dour rockiness of the surrounding land behind. Nowhere is this impression more marked, perhaps, than in the great sandy sweep of Luskintyre by the Sound of Taransay.

Machair conditions are much less a feature of mainland places, but restricted areas of wind-blown sand do provide valuable

Steep slopes, thin soils, persistent cloud and high rainfall limit the potential for land use over vast tracts of the West Highlands. (Sligachan, Isle of Skye).

well-drained croft grazings. Along such a rock-girt shore the sandy beaches are honeypots for holidaymakers. The damage done on summer days is greatly emphasised when winter gales lash the land and tear at the damaged turf. The power of the wind to shift beach sand can be dramatically seen at Invernaver on the north Sutherland coast. Winter gales can wreak havoc on damaged machair land, causing a blow-out of the sandy base. The fragility of the machair ecosystem has been demonstrated on some crofter grazings in west Sutherland where the pressures of human feet and vehicle tyres on the sandy honeypots have resulted in degradation and erosion of the vulnerable coastal sward, a loss both for crofters as good grazing land and for those who come to enjoy the seaside in a spectacular setting.

Wind is an all-pervading feature of the climate of the crofting province, its influence on the land and on human activity being evident everywhere. Trees are often conspicuous by their absence in coastal situations, and those that do grow in exposed places bend submissively away from the prevailing blasts. They have little place in the island scene. Dr I. F. Grant once recalled how an island woman visiting the mainland remarked dismissively that 'Trees are untidy looking things'.

The thatched roofs on some of the old style of crofter housing and the mobile homes which are a mark of today's housing shortages in some areas must be securely fixed for fear of strong winds. For a while, the feasibility of planting the tough and wind-resistant New Zealand flax as windbreaks was experimented with in the Outer Hebrides. But the effects are not all bad. Wind-blown sand helps sweeten the ground on which it is deposited, for it is often rich in fragments of sea shells which have a high lime content. Crushed and applied to the land, shell sand is an antidote to the high soil acidity of this high rainfall area. And in earlier times, when seaweed was so prized as a fertiliser, and even as an industrial raw material for kelp, the great banks of weed cast ashore by wild Atlantic gales were regarded as a valuable resource.

In response to the threat of unrestrained wind, Shetland crofters created deep depressions or *nousts* above the beach to fit the form of fishing boats, so that they could be out of the reach of the gales. Small island mail boats have had to be hauled laboriously out of the water to avoid the destructive

Shetland yoles drawn into sheltering nousts safe from threatening wind and sea.

force of wind-tormented seas. In present-day terms, strong winds can severely curtail inshore fishing activity and play havoc with steamer sailing schedules which, in an island situation, can mean a costly disruption to the pattern of living. Generations of crofter folk have learned to live with such trials, passing wry comment on the visible frustrations of visitors more used to the certainty of unimpeded motorway movement for whom a curtailed steamer sailing seems to be the end of the world.

The Butt of Lewis is renowned for the speed of its wind gusts, the dramatic readings obtained at its lighthouse being reported in national weather forecasts for guaranteed effect, though no doubt helping to perpetuate a common myth in more southerly quarters that the north of Scotland is a land of unrestrained wind and unrelenting rain.

Wind is merely the product of rapid air movement, and it is

moving air that is largely responsible for the high rainfall amounts which crofters have to thole. Originating far out into the western ocean, the Atlantic depressions bring with them the unwelcome weather fronts which contribute so much to the area's rainfall. The islands and west Highlands are in line to receive all the moisture that may be going. And there is an added complication, too. Moisture-charged air coming in off the Atlantic is forced into a rapid rise on meeting the higher ground of the west. This then leads to cooling of the relatively warm air, resulting in condensation and a relief rainfall effect, for things are influenced by the relief or lie of the land. As a result, Fort William has the unenviable average of almost 2000 millimetres of rainfall per year. The smaller numbers of crofts which exist in the eastern Highlands in places such as Easter Ross and the Black Isle, are much less bound by such constraints of climate, for they enjoy the comparative dryness of the rain shadow effect caused by most of the rain falling over the hills to the west.

High rainfall results in leaching of the ground, a process in which nutrients are washed away, thus further reducing soil fertility. Furthermore, rainfall is associated with cloud cover which reduces sunshine amounts and this, in turn, restricts further the choice of crops which can be grown. In this way, the farming potential of the land in the crofting province is strongly influenced by the nature of the climate which operates in it. On the other hand, some places are so low-lying that they may escape the worst excesses of Atlantic rainfall. Such is the island of Tiree whose high number of sunshine hours are as legendary as the speed of the wind gusts at the Butt of Lewis.

Misconceptions abound about the true nature of the climate of the crofting areas. Snow showers will take the place of rain if air temperatures are low enough, but days with snow lying are not that frequent in coastal areas, and even the mountains do not necessarily retain a snow covering throughout the winter. In fact, the west coast of the Highlands has average temperatures higher in winter than parts of Norfolk, for the former enjoys the milder maritime effects of the Atlantic, while the latter comes under cold continental influences, including the bitter air which has travelled over from the chilled winter lands of eastern Europe.

Strictly speaking, it is not the Gulf Stream which washes past those crofts that line the western seaboard, but rather its northerly extension, the North Atlantic Drift. Nevertheless, the effect is to raise winter sea temperatures so that air coming in from the west is milder, hence the lack of frost and the presence of the green oasis of palm trees and other exotic plants at Inverewe Garden in Wester Ross. The visitor cannot fail to be impressed by the contrast between the lushness of the garden's greenery and the stark openness of the adjacent crofting land around Loch Ewe. However, the fact is that Osgood Mackenzie, creator of the garden last century, ensured that effective windbreaks were established on the peninsula at an early stage. More than anything else, it is the strong wind that limits substantial plant growth on the exposed west coast.

So the environment in which crofters developed their distinctive pattern of land use and lifestyle along Europe's Atlantic edge is one that is strongly determined by the nature of the land, and affected by the climatic influences which operate upon it. So often, the environmental opportunity for crofting has been limited in the extreme. Yet, as long as an opportunity did exist, the folk made the most of it. As a result, crofts — or the ruined reminders of them — may sometimes be found in the most challenging of places. Likewise, the marks of old cultivation ridges still mark the landscape in some surprising situations.

Today's landscape with crofts has echoes in it of a more ancient past, as we shall see next. The crofting generations may come and go, but the context of landscape and climate in which they have lived, and continue to live, remains a challenging one.

CHAPTER 2

Echoes of the past

Though crofts and crofting as we know them today were essentially the product of a conscious decision to reshape a way of life last century, the Atlantic edge of Scotland had for centuries been peopled by folk whose living was bound by the dualism of land and sea support. In this, as in other ways, the way of life lived at the edge has echoes from a more ancient past.

Today's crofters are successors to a long line of folk who have struggled with the difficulties of maintaining a living on some of the most marginal areas on Europe's north-western perimeter. For countless generations the pattern of that living remained essentially unbroken, its driving force the need to sustain human life in a grudging environment. For the most part, the earliest dwellers have few memorials, for their lifestyle neither supported the acquisition of enduring riches nor raised up the kind of buildings that were likely to last. The plenishings of their homes went little beyond the basics required to maintain a family living, and as often as not the building materials of the houses were sod, stone and wood extracted and gathered from their immediate surroundings. In this regard, the crofters of the last century had much in common with those folk who had peopled the same land centuries, even millennia, before.

To trace early human origins of any kind is to tread a difficult path. With no written record existing, and material remains fragmentary and scarce, there are usually only the sketchiest of indications of how things might have been. Generations of archaeologists must have prayed for the good luck which was to come, quite fortuitously, during one 19th-century northern storm. Freed, in part at least, from the shroud of sand which had happed it for centuries, there suddenly appeared one wild day in 1850 a cluster of ancient habitations which gives us a remarkable insight into northern life as far back as Neolithic times.

When that fierce storm lashed the Bay of Skaill on Orkney's

west Mainland, it not only tore away the protecting cover of a great sand dune, but also ripped off the veil of uncertainty which had obscured the day-to-day domestic arrangements of the shadowy ancient folk who once had their living along the Atlantic ends.

The fact was that in largely treeless Orkney, the ordinary folk who made their living along the island shore were forced to assess the worth of all the alternatives which nature could provide. Whalebone from a stranded corpse on the beach had been dragged up to help form a roof structure to supplement the meagre local supplies of wood or driftwood. But it was the local stone which was to be the enduring substitute that shaped the material remains which were revealed.

What the gale uncovered, to the intense interest of the local laird, was a great compressed heap of midden remains. The excavations which followed were to reveal in remarkable detail life as it was lived by the area's most ancient folk. Coastal erosion later removed part of the midden and revealed more of the settlement. A sea wall was quickly erected to protect the site from the further threat of marine erosion, and the laird of Skaill's preliminary findings were then greatly extended by the archaeology of Professor Gordon Childe.

Until the excavation of the concealed remains of Skara Brae, the reconstruction of everyday scenes of prehistoric life had been, as Childe himself observed, 'a work of pure imagination'. Now things were to change quite dramatically. If the term 'Stone Age' tends to be synonymous with a lack of human sophistication, then this settlement clearly disproved it. In a way that never fails to impress the first-time visitor to the islands, the ancient Skara Brae folk had translated into stone the furnishings which would, in more favourable circumstances, have been made of wood. 'Stone Age' has indeed taken on a whole new, and decidedly literal, meaning at Skara Brae.

The whole assemblage of huts, along with their interior plenishings, was thus preserved in a unique way. When the covering blanket of sand was carefully trowelled away, it was as if a stage set had been revealed for some domestic drama from the Neolithic period. All that was missing were the players themselves: the folk who had shaped it all.

It was the fact that the local northern sandstone could split into flagstone slabs that enabled the Skara Brae folk to fashion so beautifully in stone their underground homes and connecting alleyways. Though life was lived beneath a well-seasoned midden where the all-pervading perfume of putrefaction must have been everpresent, there was certainly nothing primitive in the way the local building medium was employed.

Only the very tops of the underground dwellings would have protruded above the kitchen midden, a useful adaptation to life in a windswept island setting. Below ground level, the hut walls were low and slightly corbelled inwards. Ambries or keeping places, an integral part of the drystone walls, had their construction made possible by the easy-fitting nature of the flagstone. Interestingly, the provision of recessed keeping places in the walls was a long continued tradition in stone-built croft houses in the islands, maintaining a link with those earliest times.

At the centre of the roughly rectangular form of each hut was the hearth, the focus of life. It was the warm living heart of home and family, and doubtless possessed that same, almost mystical, significance which surrounded it in much more recent crofting days. Flanking the Skara Brae hearth were open stone boxes formed from thin slabs of sandstone set on end. Their joints may have been formed from clay, providing small water-holding tanks in which limpets might be stored, possibly as fishing bait.

There is, however, one stone-built feature above all which draws the eye as nothing else does. It is the great stone dresser, the Neolithic forerunner, perhaps, of today's kitchen units. In the solidity of their construction the dressers are matched by the massive stone beds in which the Skara Brae folk snuggled down among the heather while the solid stone walls and muffling midden heap deadened the roar of the winter gales outside.

Flanking the fronts of the beds are tall flagstone pillars whose purpose is perhaps made clearer by a description by Sir Arthur Mitchell of Hebridean crofters' box beds at the end of the 19th century.

'They usually consist simply of four rough, upright posts bound together by narrow side stretchers, on which rests a wooden bottom covered with loose straw. The two uprights

Old stone sinkers for fishing lines from the Viking settlement at Underhoull in Unst. Weights of identical type were still in use until recent times.

which are farthest from the wall often reach the rafters, and are attached to them by straw ropes. Upon these is a sort of inner roof constructed and this inner roof is often covered with divots. The need of this roof-within-a-roof depends on the fact that the outer roof is often far from water-tight. All ages and sexes occupy these beds.'

In its own way, the picture revealed by Skara Brae is strikingly similar to the one of the Northern Isles' longhouse or the Hebridean black house of last century, as described by many travellers. Moulded as much by the environment in which it was set as by the hands of the folk who fashioned it from whatever materials were available, the ancient house fulfilled the same need as those which followed it, having a range of furnishings that answered the basic requirements of family living.

But what of the life of these folk whose domestic arrangements are so much better known than they themselves? To judge by the abundance of sheep and cattle bones in the midden refuse, the Skara Brae folk must have had a strong reliance on stock keeping. The seashore would also have been an important complement to the sandy coastal strip in providing a food supply, for folk could collect shells, just as they were forced to do in days long after as a result of food shortage. Skara Brae, though separated by several thousand years from modern crofting times, would therefore suggest that those early folk had that same dual dependence on land and sea that has more recently characterised the life of crofting and other communities along the Atlantic ends of the British Isles and beyond.

Blown sand also played its part in the survival of another early settlement site, that of Jarlshof on south Mainland of Shetland. Originally known as 'Da Laird's Hoose', it became known by its present Norse name after Sir Walter Scott so described it in his novel *The Pirate*. Sand-blow from the nearby dune system, coupled with a long build-up of debris from successive occupations, had led to the growth of a great mound of material which gave archaeologists many rewarding field days while trying to reconstruct a picture of the domestic arrangements of early times.

Thus early life at the edge was very much a matter of making the most of what the environment could offer. That these early Northern Isles' folk manufactured their tools from local stone, is evident in the finding of split pebble knives and the like, much in the manner of the Skara Brae dwellers a little further to the south. Archaeological evidence paints a picture of a folk again in the same kind of tradition, in a way a kind of ancient echo of the crofting ways of folk to come, pasturing cattle and sheep on the sandy coastal turf and collecting shellfish at low tide along the voe. Driftwood would also have been a much-prized item from among the sea's largesse, as it still is for many islanders today in largely treeless environments.

The succeeding evidence sheds more light on the economy of the time. From their small dwellings among the dunes, the Bronze Age folk of Jarlshof continued to gather shellfish along

Shaped by tradition and response to the environment, the old buildings seem to spring from the ground which provided their materials. Mainland, Orkney.

the shore, as well as catching fish. Their interest, however, seems to have been more strongly in the land, for there is plenty of evidence of sheep rearing and the keeping of small cattle. The light and sandy soil supported the growing of food crops, with evidence of the cultivation of bere, the primitive form of barley grown by island crofters until present times.

In the later Bronze Age period, a series of circular stone-built houses was added to the site with souterrains or earth houses as underground storage places which would suggest the storing of perishable foodstuffs safely out of the reach of salt-drenching blasts. But the round houses of the Bronze Age do not mark the end of this remarkable sequence of occupation. Above the sand drifts which buried the earlier dwellings, a massive round tower or broch was raised up from local stone. It is clear from the accumulated evidence that the broch builders continued that same coastal tradition of dependence on coastal fringe and inshore waters. Bere was ground into meal in saddle-shaped stone querns, different in shape from those still in use among crofters last century and occasionally later, but employing the same local stone and utilising the same human effort. To the well-established husbandry of sheep and cattle was apparently added the keeping of pigs. At the same time the natural seaside harvests of seal meat and seabirds continued to add variety to the meal, meat and seafood diet just as it did in many island situations last century and even into the present. The men of Ness in Lewis uphold an ancient tradition in their yearly trip to Sula Sgeir to collect young seabirds.

Of all the stone-built relics in the crofting province, nothing fixes the attention quite like the surviving brochs. Compelling in its stature and visual attraction, the solid form of the broch is both a testimony to the enduring quality of the local stone and to the skills of the builders who shaped it, employing the well-practised art of drystone construction.

Dun Carloway in the west of Lewis stands sentinel over a crofting landscape of bare rock and peat bog where crops and cattle have had to fit in where they could. This grey stone fortification which sits brooding on its elevated site has overseen the comings and goings of countless crofter generations who must often have lifted their eyes towards its stark form, wondering at the life and times of the folk who felt impelled to raise up such long-lasting walls in defence of their ways, for the brochs are clearly fortifications.

By contrast, the most intact and imposing broch of all sits squatly by a Shetland shore. On the edge of the well-grazed turf of the island of Mousa off south Mainland this flagstone-built tower rises more than 14 metres high. Its solid form is over 16 metres in diameter at the base and 13 metres at the top. Of the 500 or so brochs identified throughout northern Scotland, Mousa ranks as the classic, eclipsing even the well-preserved fortifications of Carloway and of Glenelg in mainland Inverness-shire in the quality of its preservation. Whatever the need for their building, the brochs are remarkably similar in form wherever they occur. They may differ in the nature of their stonework depending on the geological basis of the land on which they stand, but their internal stone stairs and galleries conform to an arrangement that is remarkably unvarying.

Norse place-name derivations throughout the crofting province attest to the raiding exploits of the Vikings. Western

The ancient broch of Dun Carloway sits darkly brooding above its surrounding crofts.

island names such as Scalpay, Vatersay and Eriskay provide a parallel to northern names like Whalsay, Eday and Graemsay, each recalling the Norse *ey*, meaning island. It is, of course, in the Northern Isles and in the northernmost portion of mainland Scotland that the Scandinavian overlay is most strongly evident on the landscape and even in the speech of northern crofting folk. Nevertheless, the Norse influence which is perpetuated in so many croft place-name elements provides a common bond for areas of north and west that are often assumed to be culturally far divided.

For example, an obvious illustration would be the Gaelic word *sioman*, meaning a rope of straw or hay used on a roof or corn stack, which has its equivalent in *simmen* in Shetland and *simmonds* in Orkney. Another is *sgru'an*, the word for a corn stack in Western places from the Aird to Assynt, but which was a *skroo* to crofters storing their harvests in the Northern Isles.

The historical record does not lend much support to the popular image of blonde-haired Viking oarsmen intent on a mission of unbridled pillage and rape, but instead suggests a colonisation by land-hungry northern peasant farmers interested more in the acquisition of ground for growing crops and for pasturing cattle than in the opportunity for the meagre lootings which most places might provide.

At Jarlshof, the Viking arrival in the early 9th century left its impress in the form of the rectangular bow-shaped building plan. The archaeological record is added to by a number of later farmsteads. Their remains survive as a memorial to a period of time characterised more by peace than by pillage. In the mid 1960s, I took part in the Aberdeen University Geography Department's excavation of the Viking site at Underhoull in Unst in Shetland under the supervision of Alan Small. This revealed the concealed remains of a Norse longhouse. There, on the sloping site where those land-hungry settlers from across the North Sea established their claim to this island place, it was possible on a fine summer's evening to imagine those Norsemen engaged in the very same life-sustaining chores as the crofting folk who followed them in their fishing and land-working ways, against the same sound backcloth of sea and perhaps of plaintively whistling whimbrel as well.

The remains of iron sickle blades confirm the crop-growing activities of the time, while soapstone pot sherds are a reminder both of the material's local occurrence, and perhaps of the continued contacts of the Viking folk with their homeland, for steatite outcrops were also worked in the south-west of Norway.

With sea sounds always in the air, it would have been surprising indeed if archaeology had not uncovered evidence for a strong tradition of harvesting the resources of the sea. The abundant line and net sinkers found at sites like Underhoull and Jarlshof are almost identical to those in use by crofter-fishermen in quite recent times. They underline the importance of the sea as a resource base, and suggest that the once familiar description of a Shetlander as 'a fisherman with a croft' may indeed have had a much earlier application.

These early sites from the northern and western isles are of considerable interest. Skara Brae in Orkney, Jarlshof, and Dun Carloway in Lewis, plus a host of other well-recorded sites, provide a happy hunting ground for those who would seek out some links with today's crofting stock and their traditions. In geographical location each may be unique, but taken together they are the means of building up a general picture of the folk who had their living along the Atlantic edge all those centuries ago. And while technological progress may have resulted in improved techniques and new ways of working, it is surprising how some of that ancient past has been echoed in the continuing traditions of more recent times, as with some of the old building styles.

Of course, there is always a tendency for old ways to be regarded as, at best quaint, and at worst the expression of a backward people. Nineteenth-century travellers were wont to take this kind of view, but in the case of the crofters' culture things persisted because they had grown out of the response of the people to an environment that was essentially unchanging. That old ways lasted until recent times is therefore not so much an expression of a culture that failed to develop as of one where the old ways of doing things were time-honoured ways, tried and tested in an environment and social circumstances that frequently offered limited potential for innovation.

CHAPTER 3

Troubled times: The Origins of crofting

We may be sure that in the pulse and pattern of human life in western and northern Scotland, continuity rather than change was the general theme over long periods of time. By the 18th century, life in the Highlands and Islands was settled in a pattern of farming that aspired to self-sufficiency – but frequently did not succeed – and produced limited commercial output, supplying hardy black cattle as a source of meat for the fast-growing urban populations of the south.

But history has shown that the most ordinary of folk in the most out of the way locations are not immune to the upheavals which come in the wake of political change. In the social history of the Highlands, the year 1746 acts as a watershed. It was then, above the sweep of blue firth and distant dark profile of the Black Isle, that the English army routed the highland clans on bare Drumossie Moor on a grey April day. Today, that same battlefield of Culloden, for a time indecently clothed with the serried ranks of planted conifers, but now laid bare once more, has become a place of pilgrimage for many who would seek to renew their links with the clans which suffered such losses that day. Defeat was followed by a general government clamp-down on the Highlands, with a symbolically important ban on the wearing of clan tartans. For the Jacobite sympathisers, the uprising of 1745 was to become just a bitter memory of what might have been had Charles Edward Stuart succeeded in his purpose of claiming the throne. Unfortunately, Highland history has been all too often romanticised, not least in the story of Bonnie Prince Charlie. What was to prove more significant was the change to come in the life of the ordinary people. In the longer term, after defeat came a transformation of the whole social order. As a consequence, life in the north would never be the same again.

The clan system had long tied the people together by bonds of kinship within the geographical setting of their clan lands. But distance has lent a certain enchantment to the image of those early days. Certainly there was a fierce pride in each clan's ability to rear fighting men. They were the chief's strategic reserve, ready to take up arms at a moment's notice. In considering the clan structure, however, romance has too often been allowed to distort reality. The clan system has been portrayed as a romantic ideal in a romantic setting, but the reality in terms of ordinary lives would have been quite different.

It was a fact of clan life that the chiefs often had little direct contact with the land which fed their folk and supplied their rents. The role of clan leadership must be examined in the light of what history relates. Direct contact with the land and its people was more usually left to the tacksmen, a kind of gentleman farmer class, who let out the land to the tenants, the ones who tilled the ground and planted the seeds. The same tenants reared the hardy black cattle which Highlanders supplied to the southern markets by way of the drove roads that converged on the trysts at Crieff and Falkirk and gave the Highlands an economic output. But in this hierarchy of Highland landholding, there were even lower orders still, in particular the cottars who held their tiny patches of ground as subtenants of the small tenants.

Producing cereal crops in a climatic province where rainfall levels are high and cloud cover frequent could never be a certain way of assuring a family diet. Seed oats were yearly committed to the bare ground of the open rigs in the hope more than the certainty of a reasonable return. When a grain crop was coaxed from the grudging ground, the resulting oatmeal was a filling fare, but scarcity rather than plenty characterised its output at tenant level. Yet payments of rents were required in kind, including kain hens (often the scraggiest birds from the wife's flock) and the all-important grain, so that in poor harvest years there was no way that ordinary folk could discharge their debt.

When such a thing happened in the old days, a clan chief might be prepared to forego his rents for that year, conscious of the need to retain his people around him as a fighting force. Since food shortages were an almost permanent part of life, emergency supplies of oatmeal from more favoured highland districts and the south used up the proceeds from the cattle sales. Throughout the whole of the Highlands and Islands this was an insecure basis for the support of a population now undergoing a rapid increase. In the past whooping cough, measles and smallpox had all taken a terrible toll. Infection and contagion were a part of life within crowded, unhealthy homes. But now disease, the scourge of living in earlier times, was being brought under some control.

Inoculation was allowing the people to fight back. In Shetland the landlords often paid for inoculation schemes themselves, and the ministers who wrote their parish accounts for the New Statistical Account in the early part of last century commented on the extent to which inoculation had been introduced throughout their northern parishes. In this demographic transition away from a situation where birth and death rates both ran at a high level, infant mortality was declining, allowing more children to survive to maturity. The birth rate remained high, however, and so did family size. As each old year gave way to a new, the land was required to feed more and more mouths than ever before. For the ordinary folk of the Highlands and Islands, the living was therefore far from easy.

At the basic level of food and shelter, things were barely sufficient to sustain anything resembling a healthy lifestyle. Travellers' tales of the time are enlivened by graphic descriptions of everyday life in the Highlands at this time. The oft-quoted Captain Burt, an army engineer sent north as part of a strategic drive to improve communications to the north, was a keen observer and recorder of the Highland scene. Through his eyes we can see something of the life and times of the folk of the old farming townships. Of their abodes, he paints a picture of life lived out at a basic level in the smoky atmosphere of the house, its focus the glowing peat fire round which the folk crowded till their legs and thighs were scorched into the marbled patterns of the *breacan*.

In such a society, things did not have to go far to descend to low depths, and necessity imposed its own demands. Cattle were bled to supplement the meagre family diet when food supplies ran low, and there were doubtless many occasions when the clan chief had to tide over some of his kinsfolk with food from outside until the next harvest came round and some sort of equilibrium could be restored.

Croft at Strathy Point, North Sutherland. Here, on this windswept northern peninsula, the people cleared from the inland straths faced the challenge of creating a new living.

But that was the way things were. In the years following Culloden, however, things were to change. The clan chiefs had now donned the new mantle of laird, and the transformation was not without its difficulties. To begin with, there was the problem of the tacksmen who held the position in the hierarchy between chief and common people and who were forced now to ponder what their role might be in the changing order. For a great many the truth was an unpalatable one. With hereditary tacks at an end and the farming lands now being offered to whoever could offer the highest rent, many of the tacksmen could see no future for themselves at all, and thus there started off one of the emigrations to the New World which became such a part of Highland history in the decades that were to follow.

Since the lairds' wealth was directly linked to what his tenants could harvest from the land, the way in which that land was used was of great importance. The linked fears of inability to pay the rent and insufficiency of food to feed the family were rooted in the manner in which the land was held and its working organised. It is a feature of the Scottish rural lowlands that individual farm houses pattern the landscape, with their farming lands gathered around them in dyked or fenced fields. In marked contrast is the situation in parts of continental Europe, where the rural population pattern is still one of nucleated farm villages, with individual farm houses closely grouped together at the heart of their farmlands.

In fact, this nucleated pattern resembles the Scottish situation of earlier times, with each farming township working its surrounding land. In this arrangement, individual tenants held a number of strips scattered about the various patches of cultivation. Runrig was a wasteful and time-consuming system, particularly when the same rigs were not necessarily held from year to year by the same persons. Its justification was the fairness of allocation of different qualities of land. At the end of the harvest, all the township livestock were allowed to trample and wander at will. Against such a background, any individual incentive to improve just did not exist.

The holding of the land in runrig was a characteristic of the old Highland system of joint tenancies where a number of families shared the land and its working. A very late survival of the system was the township of Auchindrain in Argyll, now preserved as an open air museum. Even towards the end of the last century its arable strips were still being ballotted for, as they once had been throughout the Scottish rural scene.

In lowland Scotland, the latter half of the 18th century saw great transformations in the rural landscape as the lairds strove to rid the land of runrig and raise the profitability of their lands. Such was the nature of the environment of the Highlands and Islands, however, that the area could offer only limited potential for economic reorganisation. Lowland ideas for improvement may have been appropriate to the environment of the more southerly parts of the country, but in Highland terms they formed an inappropriate model for progress.

The creation of the crofting system as the northern response to rural progress was as much an innovation for the Highlands and Islands as was the move towards consolidation for the lowland farmscape. It had its origins in the same landlord motives of a desire to rationalise and to raise the level of the land's productivity. The farming folk — now to become known as crofters — were to have their lifestyles moulded into the distinctive pattern which so dominates the crofting scene today.

Now, in place of the clachans with their untidy scatter of runrig lands, was to emerge a new northern pattern of small, organised landholdings which were to mark the beginning of crofting as we know it today over vast tracts of the Highlands and Islands. Doubtless the lairds and their land surveyors viewed the changes as a policy of rationalisation; the ordinary folk more often regarded them as the harsh removal of their way of life. In creating these small tenancies, however, the landlords had more on their minds than what the small tenants might produce after runrig had gone. The vast interior tracts of the north offered great scope for the introduction of commercial sheep farming. And while nature might be grudging with the tenants' harvests of the land, their attention could be turned to other things. The harvest of the shores in the form of kelp-gathering and burning had become a profitable economic alternative. There were also fish to be caught to supplement the diet or even provide a commercial product.

Although the Highlands and Islands have lacked the natural resources upon which the great British industries were founded further south, this does not mean that the region was untouched by the 19th century wave of development which created them. Indeed, northern and western Scotland came to supply the primary products of an industrial society that was far removed from it. It was hardly surprising, then, that estate owners in the north should look towards the grazing potential of their lands for sheep rather than for the black cattle which had traditionally been produced there. The meagre rents which small tenants could pay would be eclipsed by those which sheep farmers could afford from the rich profits of the wool clip. *Na Caoraich Mhor* — the Great Sheep — would need plenty of room to become established in the kind of flock sizes that would maximise profits. Southern flockmasters, well versed in the large-scale management of sheep in southern Scotland and northern England, were only too eager to pay the high level of rents demanded for the new sheep farms, for the wool market was a buoyant one.

There was, of course, an obstacle in the way of any transition towards extensive sheep farming. The people who occupied the land which would make the best grazings were inconveniently in the way and would have to be moved. What this meant on many estates was that they were to be confined to the very edge of the land, along the coastal fringe.

Few other subjects or events in Highland history have aroused so much passion as the removal of the people from their homes in the Highland straths. When little else is recalled about the history of northern Scotland, the 'Highland Clearances' remain an emotive subject in the recollection of the nation's past. In the general perception of those times, clearance is often linked with emigration, but the short distance move from inland strath to coastal fringe, or even from one part of a valley to another, was invariably what landowners had in mind for the people who occupied their estates. Some were merely part of a localised reorganisation of the land holdings where the ground was already in cultivation, but others were expected to improve barren peat moor.

The lairds and the factors who attended to their bidding may have expected the shift of the people to have been short in terms of geography. The reality, however, was that the kind of life envisaged for them as crofter-fishers at the coast was poles apart from their traditional, close connection with the land alone.

Much ground has been covered in the portrayal and interpretation of the events surrounding the clearances to the coast that took place throughout the Highlands and Islands. But since the name of Strathnaver is popularly linked perhaps more than others with this part of the story, it might be useful to consider the events as they unfolded in that corridor of lowland that runs northwards through the upland country of Sutherland.

The Naver River rises in the inhospitable interior of the old county, flowing northwards through a fairly broad valley to enter the sea at Torrisdale Bay. Throughout its length, countless grey ruins and marks of old settlements bear witness to the fact that the strath was once quite densely populated. As elsewhere, oats and bere were produced on narrow rigs, the outlines of which persist to this day. But self-sufficiency in food production would have been more of an aspiration than a reality, and the area traditionally depended on grain imports from the more productive lowlands of nearby Caithness to avert real hunger.

The Countess of Sutherland, owner of vast estate lands in northern Scotland, acquired her title of Marchioness of Stafford when her husband succeeded to his family title in 1803. His subsequent rise in the peerage occurred when he was created Duke of Sutherland. The Sutherland family's great wealth came from the Stafford estates in England and from the Duke of Bridgewater's fortune which was derived from the southern canal system, so fundamental a part of the rapid industrialisation of the south. It was perhaps hardly surprising that they should have embraced both the idea of using their lands to produce a basic industrial raw material to supply the hungry weaving looms of the south, and also of encouraging their tenants, as they saw it, into something resembling a more industrial model of livelihood along the coastal edge.

The first clearance from Strathnaver began when an enormous sheep farm was created in 1806. This involved the removal of families from the upper part of the valley, though most of them were accommodated in townships no great distance away on the other side of Loch Naver. This undoubtedly would have caused severe problems of over-population, for the land could barely support those who worked it already.

A few years later, the name of Patrick Sellar, assistant estate factor, begins to assume some prominence in the historical record as a prime mover in the forced removal of the population. In 1813, trouble had flared up at Kildonan when popular resistance to the coming of the big sheep was met by the strength of the law and by the military force sent up from Fort George. The people to be cleared from the strath were not prepared to accept the alternative lands offered to them on the exposed coast. The Kildonan Riots demonstrated that the people were far from willing participants in the estate's plans for reorganisation of their lives and living pattern. But this land of their ancestors was not theirs by law, and the strength of the law was more powerful than their resistance. So the insurrection was quelled, and Patrick Sellar proceeded with his purpose. In addition to his estate duties, his interest in the lands of the strath was, however, a more personal and vested one, for he had himself become tenant of a large Strathnaver sheep farm.

To a people rooted to their land in practices of working which can have changed little for generations, the prospect of resettlement and adoption of a different lifestyle can have had little appeal. Their reluctance to move was therefore hardly unexpected. In 1814 the legal process of eviction from Strathnaver began once more. Roofs were removed from dwellings, and in some cases their timbers burned to prevent any possibility of reoccupation. But there was more to the resistance to removal than just an inbuilt reluctance to shift. The new allotments or crofts on the coast were not yet ready to receive a displaced population. Understandably, the folk were unwilling to move to an unknown future.

The grievances of the people could hardly be ignored by the Staffords in their grand castle home overlooking the Moray Firth, for there were sorry reports of destruction of houses and outbuildings, damage to standing crops and deliberate burning of pasture land that portrayed Sellar in the worst possible light. More serious by far was the accusation that he had caused the death of an old woman who died shortly after being evicted from the house of her son-in-law. Patrick Sellar was brought to court in Inverness, but was acquitted of the charges brought against him and returned to further his ideas for the estate.

If Patrick Sellar had wrought social havoc in Strathnaver, James Loch who came to be an important manager of the Sutherland estate and Francis Suther, the new factor, were to add to the impress on the landscape of the north by a continuing clearance policy. Conscious of the bad image created by past evictions, Loch was anxious to adopt a more low-key approach, though his proposals were no less radical. Families were to be cleared from the interior lands of Armadale to the exposed and inhospitable Strathy Point at a veritable land's end of the north coast.

Resistance to notice of removal in May of 1819 was met with a firm response. Nearly 200 houses were cleared in Strathnaver in that year. At times, roof timbers and thatch were set alight and walls pulled down to discourage any notion of a return by the displaced families. Denied of the precious roof supports, the building of new homes would thus be even more of a problem.

Islanders removed from the better lands of western Harris were forced to take a living from the inhospitable eastern fringe.

Decades later, the simmering bitterness of the people at the manner of their removal was to surface at the Napier Commission hearings at Bettyhill. Angus Mackay, a crofter's son from Farr, voiced the feelings of the local crofting community — essentially a community of displaced people — when he told the Commissioners:

> 'We and our fathers have been cruelly burnt like wasps out of Strathnaver, and forced down to the barren rocks of the sea-shore, where we had in many cases to carry earth on our backs to form a patch of land.'

The resettlement of the Strathnaver people took place in a chain of coastal townships from the river mouth eastwards to Portskerra. In line with estate policy, allotments of land were small in the extreme, as Patrick Sellar himself noted:

> '. . . in lots under the size of three arable acres, sufficient for the maintenance of an industrious family, but pinched enough

to cause them to turn their attention to fishing.'

In a sense, the people found themselves in the same position as those in some countries of the developing world in more recent times, where such things as flooding of river valleys for water storage and hydro-electricity schemes have forced the people to resettle in much less productive farming areas. But whereas expensive re-training schemes have in some measure converted the people there to a more fishing-based economy, the Strathnaver crofters were expected to get on with the business of transforming themselves into fishermen with no outside assistance. On the contrary, there were actually major obstacles in the way of development of the local fishing. A serious complaint was of the want of a proper harbour on such an exposed stretch of coastline, and of the further difficulty of having to compete with the larger boats based in the proper harbours of the east coast.

With no such thing as Social Security or any manner of support, destitution never dwelt far from the townships. Hunger was an ever present scourge of life along the north coast. In time, succeeding generations did become crofter-fishers, but the estate's idea of the speedy conversion of a farming people to a fishing workforce along Scotland's northern edge never came to fruition.

Perhaps understandably, attention has often been concentrated on Sutherland, a county which saw the widespread displacement of its inland population to the coast. The events surrounding the Sutherland evictions may have been dramatic and well dramatised by succeeding generations, but the fact is that crofting communities from Shetland in the north to the mainland edge and Hebrides in the west have their own histories of removal of forebears to form new crofting settlements. Weisdale, Rousay, Raasay, Glenelg, Morvern, Mull, Islay . . . . The names form a long litany of the homelands of the dispossessed.

Clearance and eviction are emotive terms upon which the history of the Highlands has often focused. But they are just a part of a human story whose lasting impress is, above all, the crofting townships which remain such a distinctive part of Scotland's rural scene.

CHAPTER 4

Troubled Times: Feasts and Famine

Along the low western shores, underwater forests of seaweed line the coastal edge. Valued for years as the main provider of fertility for the land, the great banks of weed cast up by the Atlantic gales were laboriously carried by cart and creel from the shore and spread over the ground. But now the sea's largesse was to be converted into a fortune for the lairds who came even to grudge their tenants the time-honoured use of the weed as fertiliser for growing their crops.

Kelp was an alkaline ash, the residue from burning large quantities of weed on the shore. Its main use was in the manufacture of glass and soap products in southern factories. For northern lairds, the seemingly insatiable demand for the product was manna from heaven. Here was an industry which was based on an abundant and free natural resource, and one which could be widely supported wherever seaweed could be obtained in sufficient quantity. What was more, the resource was a renewable one, for the seaweed kept on growing after it had been cut.

The potential for making money on estates having the optimum conditions of low-shelving shores seemed endless. Practically no capital investment was required. The tools of the kelp cutters, who sometimes had to wade up to their necks in the cold Atlantic to cut the growing tangles, were simple metal hooks. Neither were expensive ovens or furnaces needed for the burning process, and the combustion of the weed was easily achieved in a simple stone-lined pit with the aid of the sea breezes to fan the flames.

In northern terms, the story of the kelp industry really had its origins in the Northern Isles. In 1722, James Fea introduced kelp burning into the Orkney island of Stronsay where it was said that 'to the eye of a passing mariner the smoke from the kilns gave it the appearance of an active volcano'. In the canny minds of ordinary island folk, the new practice was viewed with much suspicion. The smoke was alleged to be a danger to human and animal health, as well as the cause of bad harvests.

But the prejudice was soon overcome. For the lairds, the attraction of such a high-value, low-capital pursuit was irresistible. By mid-century the smoking fires of the kelp burners had also spread along the shores of the Western Isles, some of which, like the Uists and Benbecula, were especially well placed to exploit the rich seaweed resources around their coasts.

For the ordinary folk who put so much physical effort into collecting and burning the seaweed, the financial rewards were paltry when set beside the vast profits accruing to the lairds. Estates with good kelp shores could hardly fail to make money, but it was a labour-intensive employment which hinged on the certain availability of a seasonal work force. In this regard the lairds had a trump card to play. By providing their crofter tenants with highly restricted allocations of land, they could ensure that their work force were obliged to earn more to help towards the payment of rents. Thus there came into being that thirlage in which the lairds firmly held their crofting tenantry, all the time ensuring their own steady and substantial profits.

In economic terms, kelp making came to line the pockets of the lairds along hundreds of Hebridean shores, across to the rocky edge of the western mainland, north through the Orkney archipelago, and up into Shetland. These were boom days along the northern shores, and every area that could produce kelp was made to do so. Though the broken Shetland coast, for example, was physically far from favourable for kelp making, such was the push to profit from the industry that burning still took place at scattered sites from Sumburgh in the south to Unst in the north, though most of these northernmost shores were poorly suited to it.

In social terms, it is a fact of history that kelp making shaped the lives of the people, and even dictated the ways in which the land was divided. In the predictable pattern of underdeveloped places, the people laboured for a pittance to produce a valuable primary product for export, while their employers lived in style off the fruits of the tenants' labours. Crofting and kelp burning therefore came to be inextricably bound together for the lairds' good, but the tragedy was that the accruing of such wealth would ultimately be the cause of their tenants' severe want.

Even manipulating the demographic circumstances of the time was not above some of the lairds, for in their encouragement of early marriages to ensure large families, and thus a supply of workers, they succeeded in increasing the birthrate. In Shetland, too, the lairds saw the potential for tying crofting to a more lucrative partner pursuit. In this case it was the *haaf* or deep sea fishing, prosecuted by men from crofts that were hopelessly undersized and unable to provide for a family's support. Further subdivision of already inadequate holdings helped increase the workforce. At the same time it put the population well beyond the capacity of the land to support it, and therein lies a definition of overpopulation.

Throughout the crofting province as it had now become, the strategy had its desired effect. Crofters unable to make a living from their land alone were forced to toe the landowner's line and burn his kelp or catch his fish. Inevitably, the value of many estates came to be counted more in terms of what the shoreline and offshore waters could produce than in what the land might yield. Yet the land was the people's basic and time-honoured support, and any failure of that support was bound to spell disaster. When changed market conditions cut the demand for Scottish kelp, boom was followed by bust, and hunger and starvation were the unhappy result. The landlords' rich feastings in the days of plenty were to have their cruel antithesis in the days of famine which were to follow.

To think of famine today is perhaps to conjure up television images of third world countries where the shadow of starvation and death hovers disturbingly near. But we relax comfortably in our living rooms in the knowledge that such things are reassuringly far removed from our shores. To contemplate such a tragedy on our own doorstep would be to think the unthinkable. Yet the Highlands and Islands last century closely resembled the situation of those countries whose problems we all too often see on our television screens today. The plain fact is that as recently as last century, food shortages and even famine itself were no rare events, but part of the way of life for vast numbers of Scotland's crofting population.

To seek the reason, we must remember that interplay of physical and socio-economic factors that shaped the way in which people worked the land. In other words, the nature of the landscape, the climate, and the way the croft land was used were all important strands in the fabric of the crofters' story in the past. Within the crofting areas, satisfactory food-producing land was limited both in distribution and in quality. In addition, geographical isolation imposed the need to strive for self-sufficiency. People required adequate food to survive and to provide the energy for work. Laird and tacksman therefore had a vested interest in the output of the land, for it was the means by which the rents were discharged.

Runrig had imposed its own limits on productivity, but given a reasonable growing season and a plentiful supply of seaweed fertiliser, communities could at least aspire towards self-sufficiency. The yield of a cereal crop such as oats or bere, as we have already noted, is governed by the vagaries of the weather. At the same time, local conditions could vary widely. In one part there might be sufficiency and in another a shortage severe enough to threaten starvation. At national level, famine in a remote Scottish community might be dismissed as a minor local difficulty, but for a desperate people it was real enough, and enforced diets of nettles, weed seeds and shellfish from the shore were common antidotes to hunger.

On the whole, Shetlanders appear to have had a better diet than their fellow crofters along the western seaboard. The northern waters were productive of fish, and cabbages were widely propagated in the little stone-built planticrues. Thus the diet was a rather more balanced and nutritious one than most Hebridean crofters were used to.

With population throughout the north reaching record levels and more and more people being forced to survive on smaller and smaller patches of ground as subdivision took place, the situation could only get worse. Only the near monoculture of a more reliable crop than grain could ever have supported the population. The tuberous potato was a native of South America where peasant farmers had long planted it on the mountain slopes. It had come to Britain first by way of the American colonies and became the absolute staple in the west of Ireland. That it became equally entrenched as a food crop in the Highlands and Islands is a measure both of the crop's versatility and of the vital importance of a reliable staple that would support the people.

Sheep dyke, North Ronaldsay. The massive drystone dyke confines the common grazings to the island shore.
In days when profits from kelp burning were high, the island shorelines were often valued more than the land itself.

As early as the mid-18th century the stage had been set for the diffusion of the potato throughout the Highlands. Initially there had been no great enthusiasm for such an unappetising-looking root. Indeed, there was that same consumer resistance to novel food crops in the Highlands and Islands that is experienced still in some rural areas of the world. Such reluctance to welcome a crop with so much food-producing potential may seem strange from our perspective in time, but in a situation where family life depended so directly on the production of sufficient food from the land, it is perhaps not hard to see why communities displayed such conservatism. To take any kind of step away from the well-tried staple was to take a chance with the family's food supply.

Innovation was best encouraged through practical demonstration, and it was frequently left to the parish minister to show on his own glebe lands the feeding potential of the novel root.

The Reverend William Mackenzie of the Sutherland parish of Assynt wrote of his flock — somewhat patronisingly — that:

> 'The Natives were indifferent but later their scruples were overcome and it became increasingly popular, so that in 1794 they frequently take in new land from the moor and plant them with potatoes.'

It is said that by 1790, of all the parishes of the Scottish mainland, only one, Ardersier in Inverness-shire, had not adopted the potato. Significantly, starvation had come to this same parish in the bad year of 1782 when the grain crop failed. Sometimes sheer desperation with local circumstances forced people to adopt potatoes as a food crop. This was so, for example, in the Easter Ross parish of Nigg when the all-important herring shoals disappeared from the nearby waters, resulting in a severe food shortage. So potatoes and kelp together had become the life support for thousands of people around island and mainland shores.

In the early 1820s, the stage was set for a drastic change, as kelp making faced real financial trouble. The duty levied on its preferred alternative, imported Spanish barilla, was greatly lowered and the economic advantage which Scottish kelp had enjoyed was now ruinously removed. The great labour forces, which the lairds had so assiduously fostered, suddenly lost their *raison d'être*. The people were pawns in a game whose rules were dictated by economic expediency. If it did not suit the lairds' purpose to retain such a redundant labour force where it was, then there was nothing to stop them moving it around. Removal and exodus were fated to become the order of the day, but in the meantime, the folk had to support themselves as best they could.

From our point in time, we can see how things had been shaping up for trouble. So great had dependence on the potato become that any threat to its continuing support of the people was bound to herald disaster. In 1835 an early warning of trouble came in the form of poor weather conditions throughout the Highlands, resulting in near failure of the crop on the already hard-pressed croft lands. But still the dependence continued, and the census of 1841 confirmed that the population level was higher that it had ever been before.

Disaster was waiting in the wings, and the people were the unhappy players in the unfolding tragedy.

The same destructive disease that so blighted the Irish potato crop and caused such widespread human suffering eventually came across the sea to Scotland. Its cause was carried unseen in the sea air, but its effects were all too obvious. In 1845 the disease caused serious damage to the crop throughout Scotland, though many northern districts were fortunate in escaping its worst ravages. It was the following season that was to go down in the annals as the year of the great potato famine, a year when the peril of such out-and-out dependence on one staple crop was to be demonstrated in human misery on a scale previously unseen. In the damp air of that fateful summer, the fungus spores were able to work their worst. Within weeks, healthy potato shaws were blighted beyond recovery, and crofters everywhere could only watch in dread as their food supply died and decayed before their eyes.

The old runrig farming style with its inefficient methods of crop and cattle production may often have been beset by local difficulties of disease and failure, but the sheer scale of the potato calamity in the crowded crofting communities was a different experience altogether and touched the national conscience. Money was raised and converted to famine relief in the form of oatmeal sent to crofting areas from Scotland's big cities and from church members' givings. The Highland Relief Board dispatched many cargoes of oatmeal by sea to alleviate suffering.

In places, an attempt was made to turn disaster to some advantage by giving crofters paid employment in digging ditches to drain their lands. It may be difficult to recognise the results of their labours in the landscape today, but in several parts of the Highlands there are still tangible reminders of those terrible times past in the form of the 'destitution' roads built by working men in return for the relief food aid which they received for their families.

Here now was a fresh opportunity for some of the landed clan chiefs to demonstrate a practical concern for their clansfolk. Some seemed singularly unmoved by the plight of their people, however, though others responded to their needs. On Skye, the MacLeod of MacLeod carried out what relief works he could for the crofters on his land, but such was the scale of the problem that when conditions of starvation were at their worst, the despairing folk of Dunvegan called for the unfurling of the fabled fairy banner of the MacLeods in an attempt to stave off disaster.

Others were not so lucky. If people had suffered scarcity and privation before, it was as nothing compared to the scale of the potato famine. Communities were forced to contemplate the unthinkable — consuming their precious seed corn for the following year, so desperate was their immediate need. Herrings, which along with potatoes, provided the nutritious combination of *buntat' 'us sgadan*, could offer some contribution to the crofters' diet, but their shoaling was often erratic. The white fish which swam in the deeper waters offshore went largely uncaught by west coast and Hebridean crofters for want of proper boats and equipment. For many, the only marine resources that could be effectively exploited were the cockles, limpets, razor shells and whelks which were so assiduously gathered at low tide along the seashore in times of trouble.

Though 1846 stands out as a year without parallel in its problems, hunger was not to go away in the short term. The following years were also to be years of want. The pangs of hunger had been felt throughout the Highlands and Islands. Crofting, as it had been created by the lairds, had shown itself to be hopelessly ill-equipped to feed an enlarged population in hungry times.

CHAPTER 5

The making of the townships

In creating the multitude of new small crofting tenancies along the coastal fringe, the landlords often had more on their minds than what the tenants' allocation of land might produce, as we have already seen. New, planned settlement layouts were in fashion and found expression, for example, in the establishment of the fishing village of Ullapool in Wester Ross by the gentlemen directors of the British Fisheries Society. The flat, well-drained site on the raised delta at the mouth of the Ullapool river gave great scope for settlement planning in a location which also provided a sheltered harbour and easy access to good fishing grounds, though the herring which frequented them could be notoriously fickle in their appearance.

By 1788, a start was being made to the new fishing base, and the planners had to address the all-important matter of precisely how much land should be allotted to each family. Several factors had to be taken into account, not least the fact that Highlanders were well used to making do with the minimum of agricultural output in the support of their families. There was the danger also that, if they were given too much land, they might expend their energies on their ground to the exclusion of fishing which was, after all, the purpose of establishing the new settlement. In the conception and earliest growth of the village, can be detected that desire to direct the attention of the settlers seawards, thereby forcing them into a dependence on both sea and land. In the event, each family was given sufficient ground for a house and kail yard in which vegetables could be grown, along with access to ground where the all-important corn and potato crops could be raised.

To view Ullapool today from the hill above the village is to look down on a scene which has all the hallmarks of a planned settlement in the grid plan layout of its oldest part. Even today, within the earliest part of the village, a few last reminders of the old ways can be seen in the vestiges of early land demarcation and in the remnants of stone-built byres that have escaped the progressive reshaping of the settlement into its modern role as tourist centre and ferry terminal for the Western Isles.

Settlement planning was therefore becoming part of the area's development strategy of the time. It is clear also that the maritime resources of the Highlands and Islands were frequently perceived to have far more potential than the output of the land. Crofting had a very significant place in this perception. To regard it merely as one of the distinctive farming systems of Europe would therefore be quite wrong. Crofting was conceived then – and remains today – as a way of life with the land as its anchor, but whose support was, and still is, firmly based on extra-farming pursuits.

In the process of establishing new rural settlement patterns, the township was the identifiable unit on the maps of the planners. It is the crofting township above all else that puts the stamp of individuality on the human landscape of the Atlantic edge. To understand the past, we may begin with profit in the present, and particularly by looking at those striking landscape patterns of croft and croftland which contribute so distinctively to the Scottish country scene. The low houses and sharply demarcated holdings are the tangible expressions of the crofting townships in countless settings throughout the north and west. Each differs in physical and social character from its neighbour and each has its distinctive name, thus conferring upon its occupants a sense of individuality while living within a township pattern of strong uniformity. Postal addresses bear witness to the way in which every croft in a township is identified by its particular number, like 42 Arnol on Lewis's west coast, perhaps the best known croft address today because of its association with the preserved blackhouse.

The term 'township' does have different connotations in different parts of the world. But here it refers to the basic unit of land settlement: the cluster of houses with their accompanying allocations of land. Viewed from the air, crofting townships are often visually arresting features. Their straight line strips and frequently linear settlement forms draw the eye in a way that many other rural landscapes do not. In their uniformity of design and regimentation of form they contribute a strong element of order to a setting of physical diversity.

While owing much to the nature of the natural environment,

Sandwiched between sea and hill, the orderly form of the crofting landscape dominates much of Scotland's Atlantic edge. Peinachorran township, the Braes, Skye.

human activity having to fit in where it can in a landscape of such limited opportunity, the townships represent planned settlement units whose essential pattern was dictated by the measuring line and ruler of the surveyors who committed their plans to paper early last century. As Professor James Caird has noted, the restructuring of small tenant farms into crofting townships took place after precise land surveys were carried out. He has also drawn attention to the fact that the men who carried out the surveys were not from the Highlands but from the Lowlands of Scotland, probably carrying out their tasks in the better days of summer, with little appreciation of the more difficult weather conditions of the other seasons which really set the limits on land productivity.

The north coast provides some striking illustrations. The long string of settlement that marks the eastward side of Strathy Point is on an elevated situation that is open to all the unrestrained blasting of bitter Arctic air, and lashed by sea spray from the breakers in the bay below. As Angus Mackay, an 80-year-old crofter from Strathy Point told the Napier Commission hearing at Bettyhill:

> 'Strathy Point is two miles in length on one side and three upon the other. The westerly wind blows upon it, the north-west wind blows upon it, the north wind blows upon it, the north-east wind blows upon it; and when a storm comes it blasts the croft, and the people have no meat for the cattle or for themselves.'

Other nearby townships like Baligill were also open to all the fury of the north wind, an environmental difficulty that must have been a real trial for folk moved from the sheltered inland straths.

The detailed allotment plans which the surveyors produced are striking for their exactness and total regimentation of boundary lines. Yet they seem strangely out of place in the kind of environment in which they are set. Such geometric patterns of land settlement seem more in tune with the really low-lying landscapes of Europe, like the planned flat Dutch polders, than with the broken terrain of the Scottish Highlands. To visit the actual places to which the plans refer is, however, to sense that it was all somehow rather too neat, for there are places within the allotting plans where the unevenness of the land really defies such orderly demarcation. Other contemporary plans show each allotment with a neat little matching cottage, but the reality was that only the land was involved in the allocation process. The people had to shoulder the responsibility of building their own homes.

This strong uniformity of planning is a constant reminder that these crofting townships do not represent any ancient settlement pattern, but rather a conscious attempt at the beginning of the last century to accommodate a displaced people into new and highly restricted settings. The result is the repeated pattern of rectangular landholdings and individual small dwelling houses which dominates the crofting scene today.

It is not always clear just how the new crofts came to be apportioned. In some instances the matter may have been decided by drawing lots for the new allocations. Elsewhere, tenants had to accept the lotting plan imposed on them from above. Sometimes there was just insufficient 'good' ground to go round. Tenants displaced from nearby farms found themselves having to share the land with other families removed from different parts of the landowner's estate. Some families were settled on difficult virgin land which had known neither plough nor spade before, with no option but make the best of things and press on with the challenge of land reclamation.

This was the age before wire fences. In areas where the legacy of the Ice Age was a scoured and boulder-strewn surface, the materials for land division were readily available, and croft lands could be delineated by drystane dykes. The surplus stones could be used in building work or simply gathered into the clearance heaps which are the long-lasting reminder of the toil of succeeding crofter generations. Where stones were not readily available, effective land division was a problem, as on the sandy island of Tiree where impermanent turf dykes had to suffice. In fact, in more favourable environments such as Tiree, crofting was established on land with far more potential than was the case in many other situations. However, the pressures of an increasing population tended to cancel out the possible benefits of greater land capability, and in one instance a threefold increase was made over the original proposal when the crofts actually came to be allotted.

Unfortunately, such was the pressure of population increase, and the understandable reluctance on the part of crofters to see close members of their families distressed for want of land on which to grow their food, that subdivision became the order of the day, putting even further pressure on to a system of landholding already constrained by the limited nature of the original allotments. Congestion became a real and pressing problem of the coastal townships.

The way in which the crofting landscape was laid out in the early part of the last century has been a subject of interest for many scholars. E. Mairi Macarthur, in her fascinating study of the crofting community of Iona, has detailed the allotment of its crofts between 1802 and 1804. At that time, 30 rectangular holdings were laid out in the better land of the 'waist' and northern part of the island, giving the usual, starkly geometric pattern in contrast to the intervening tracts of common grazings.

Professor Caird has made a study of the laying out of crofting townships in North Uist, Wester Ross and on the north coast. As a result of the creation of crofts in North Uist, the rental rose by as much as 27%. In Gairloch the crofts have an unusually square configuration, but here, as in Sutherland, it seems that most of the former tenant farmers obtained new crofts, and that there was a significant increase in the crop-growing area as a result of land reclamation.

Without a reasonable allocation of land for common grazings, there was no way in which livestock could be kept on the crofts. Yet, provision of such vital land varied enormously. In places the grazings were reasonably extensive, but elsewhere, as in Knoydart and Glenelg in Inverness-shire, the harshness of the clearance was made worse by the very restricted allocation of the grazing land given to the crofters.

Sutherland, which saw some of the most widespread clearance resettlement, has the impressive chain of resettlement townships along its northern seaboard which have already been mentioned. A century and a half and more since their settlement, it is striking just how much of the township pattern has survived intact. Dr Frank Bardgett, the present parish minister, has commented on this strong continuity with the past in the township of Strathy West, a township created out of the more favourable and less exposed Strathy Mains farming lands a short distance from the windswept crofts on the Strathy peninsula. In this location the difficulty of providing a living in the new land allotments is demonstrated by allotment Number 2 which, although it was a little over ten acres in total area, had only three acres reckoned as arable land, the real key to family survival through crop production.

For the visitor to the north, there can be no greater indication of the change the folk had to endure, or of the difference between these new settlement forms and the old, than is revealed by a visit to one of the cleared settlements in Strathnaver, such as Achanlochy or Rosal, after one to a resettlement township on the coast. The moss- and lichen-covered ruins at the two empty sites bear silent testimony to the clearance of the strath last century when the townships supported many farming families.

Rosal was well studied by Dr Horace Fairhurst who surveyed and excavated the settlement remains which lie within the

Crofting township in the north of Lewis. The density of housing here contrasts markedly with the empty farmscapes of eastern England where agricultural improvements have displaced the rural populations.

crumbled remains of an outer ring dyke. The picture which has emerged is of three loose clusters of settlement around the interior arable land. Here the marks of the old cultivation rigs still persist as a reminder of the last efforts of the folk in producing a crop from the land. The houses themselves were of the characteristic longhouse type, with beasts' byre and people's living quarters joined together. The associated barns and corn-drying kilns complete the picture of a settlement which is quite haphazard in form. In sharp contrast to the old clachans of Rosal and Achanlochy, the coastal townships are bounded by the straight lines that are the hallmark of the planned resettlement schemes which spawned the crofting townships.

The recurring theme of rectangular land allotment dominates the face of the crofting landscape. Despite the passage of time, the amalgamation of crofts and the disuse of original boundaries, the lines of the old land allocations are still deeply etched upon the face of the land. As a result, the layout of the townships can sometimes be quite dramatic. The fan-like arrangement of the croft lands around Village Bay on the St Kildan island of Hirta has a striking pattern of narrow strips radiating outwards and widening towards the backing hill, with the township houses like a string of beads half way up to the head dyke which marks the start of the common grazings.

This is a pattern seen in other, more accessible, situations too, and is a marked feature of the west side of Lewis. The 1:25.000 Ordnance Survey map of a location like Fivepenny Borve is a fascination to look at, with its arresting patterns of long, rectangular landholdings. The plan of the township of Arnol to the south-west can be seen to follow similar lines, its long, narrow strips radiating seawards from the string of dwellings at the head of the inbye land, with the cultivated ground lying close to each croft house. The result is that the strips broaden slightly towards the shore, being at their narrowest close to the homes of the people. Beyond the line of the Arnol houses, the symmetry is broken by irregular patches taken in from the black ground beyond the township head dyke. It is no unusual thing, in fact, to find the surveyor's perfect pattern disrupted by the reclamation efforts of squatters driven by land hunger to settle out on the common grazings.

A changing sequence of crofting settlement is sometimes another feature of the human landscape pattern. This can be traced from ground remains or aerial photographs. At Arnol, all that existed earlier last century was a cluster of crofts on the machair above the shore. Later, the croft houses were moved inland. In fact, there might be an element of literal truth in such a statement, for roof timbers and lintel stones were prized possessions which might find a use in several different dwellings through time. Indeed, in the world of crofting generally, recycling can hardly be said to be a recent concept.

The new Arnol settlement was formed in the straggling line along the road that is such a characteristic of this, as of so many other townships. In a time of improving land communication, the road was the logical location for the new dwellings, providing an easy means of contact among the township folk and also an improved connection with the outside world, whether in the shape of the next township or of Stornoway, the island's urban centre. Indeed, this type of move a short distance inland from an original site near the shore is nothing unique in Lewis. It is

The Shetlander was often described as a 'fisherman with a croft'. Here fish are hung and laid out to dry in the island wind.

repeated at the township of Shawbost for the same sort of reasons of expanding population and the urge to maximise the use of scarce land.

In the rectangular strips of their allotments running back from sea to hill, crofts often had a sequence of land use from shoreline up through inbye land to the croft house and the outbye before the hill dyke marked off the common grazing beyond the township. Naturally, physical features impose a constraint on the layout of many townships. Sometimes a group of croft houses huddle together at the break of slope between low-lying land and hill, preserving the precious flatter ground for arable cultivation.

The crofting landscapes of the Northern Isles may differ in their appearance from the severely regimented patterns of the west, yet though the settlement may be dispersed around the island edges and along the shores of the voes, the same familiar pattern of houses and outhouses with small cultivation rigs on the inbye land is immediately recognisable. The strong Norse cultural overlay, however, gives its own sense of distinctiveness. The common grazings of Shetland are known by the old Norse name of *scattald*, and croft names like Dalsetter, Isbister and Flugarth preserve the memory of the Viking settlement.

Today's crofting townships therefore have their origins in the conscious decision to provide large numbers of families with small units of land which they could call their own in a way that the runrig system did not allow. Though the old system recognised the need for fairness in sharing crop-growing land that could vary greatly in quality and location, it was hardly geared towards maximising output. For a start, the lands had not been enclosed, so that any livestock not out on the common grazings beyond the head dyke had to be tethered or constantly herded, and at the end of the harvest the hill gates were thrown open to allow all the beasts to trample through the farmlands at will. With everybody's livestock on the loose, selective breeding for improvement of type stood no chance at all.

In the eyes of the lairds, a system of individual land allotment would create an incentive to produce more from the land to pay increased rents. At the same time, the restricted nature of the land allocation would act as an encouragement to the crofters to work at the industries of kelp making. In Shetland, sub-divided units of land were given to men whose labours were required at the deep sea fishing for cod and other white fish. This gave rise to the once familiar description of a Shetlander as a fisherman with a croft, the order of priority being significant.

The crofting townships therefore reflect not only a relationship with the physical geography of the areas where they occur, but also act as a commentary on the changes that were taking place in the social geography of the last century when large numbers of folk were settled on the land in units of living and working that were never meant to allow self-sufficiency from the land alone. To view the townships, therefore, as agricultural settlements of a distinctive type is not correct. Rather they represent the tangible impression upon the landscape of a distinctive way of life created to meet the circumstances of a particular time in the area's history.

CHAPTER 6

Leaving the land

In the social history of the Highlands, movement of the people has been a prime theme. Indeed, the origin of crofting itself involved the reshaping of the settlement pattern, leaving some areas entirely bereft of their people.

But even before the great overseas emigrations which are so often associated with the history of the Highlands and Islands, the people were no strangers to the idea of population movement, albeit on a seasonal or temporary basis. There was, for example, a substantial movement of men away from northern and western communities to the Caithness and east coast fisheries, placing the responsibility of land working at home firmly on the shoulders of the women. Many — including large numbers of young women — were drawn to the harvest fields of lowland Scotland as a seasonal workforce at a time when harvesting was highly labour-intensive. The areas of widespread grain cultivation in the more favoured lowland agricultural areas demanded a casual labour force that could be relied upon to appear when the corn was due to be cut. They travelled from one geographical extremity to another; from parishes of the far north-west to the harvest fields of the Lothians in Scotland's south-east. The contrast in what the land of such favoured parts could yield must have seemed great indeed, and the more so for those who journeyed in search of seasonal harvest work in the aftermath of the great failure of the potato harvests in their home areas in the 1840s.

Additionally, some were drawn from more accessible parts of the west Highlands to labour in the industries of the Central Belt, such as the dye works of Glasgow. Such seasonal movements were therefore a response to life in an environment of limited opportunity at a time when increasing population levels were imposing an additional strain on living in the Highlands and Islands generally. To think of the people living out their lives in isolated and introverted communities is therefore not necessarily correct, for many were no strangers to other parts of their country.

But such movements, great though they must often have seemed to youngsters never before away from their township homes, and of necessity undertaken on foot, were at least within the boundaries of their native country. For many, the horizons were to be very much wider, as the considerable history of highland emigration shows.

After Culloden, emigration became a significant feature of the population geography of the Highlands and Islands, though it had less to do with Jacobitism *per se* than with the changing social and demographic circumstances of the region. Commercialism was in the air. The notable northern illustration of this was the development of the town of Cromarty in the Black Isle. In fact, it could be said that as far as any kind of industrial revolution was concerned, Cromarty was the Highlands' localised centre.

During the 18th century, the small port had endured great fluctuations of fortune. William Forsyth, a well-to-do merchant then set about reviving Cromarty's flagging economy. Kelp was burned along the shores and the spinning of linen was introduced from the south. Forsyth's successor as laird in 1772 was George Ross who built on the earlier successes. The harbour was improved and trade stimulated. The manufacture of hemp rope and sailcloth was established, and imported iron was turned into nails and spades. A substantial brewery was erected, and instructors from the south brought the skills of lace making. These were boom days for the Black Isle burgh, and in the manner of burgeoning industrial centres everywhere, an outside workforce was required. This unusual pull factor of paid industrial employment induced Gaelic-speaking families from other parts of the Highlands to settle in the town. To meet their spiritual needs, the laird built a church to provide services in their native language.

Glasgow also developed its highland congregations with their worship in Gaelic, a reminder that enormous numbers of northern folk were in time drawn from their homeland to make a new life in Scotland's industrial heartland. In the story of the movement of people out of the Highlands and Islands, overseas emigration inevitably dominates because it was such a dramatic phenomenon. But the numbers who never left their native country should not be underestimated, for they came to represent a massive population shift. Urban areas of the lowlands are peppered today with the descendants of folk who moved south in search of new beginnings.

All over the north, the lairds were taking a fresh look at the potential of their estate lands for generating wealth, with an obvious expectation of higher rents. Many of the tacksmen, resentful of the change imposed upon them, and rather than submit to the new financial demands, were prepared to give up their tacks and seek a new life in more promising circumstances. There thus began the drain of the tacksmen class to the North American colonies. With them went substantial numbers of their tenants also, so that by the early years of the 1770s North Carolina had become the new home for many hundreds of Highlanders. Not unnaturally, there was some alarm at home at the exodus of so many tacksmen along with the not inconsiderable wealth they possessed, but the push factors of changing economic circumstance and increased financial demand were powerful enough to evoke this drastic response. At the same time, the pull of availability of land in a new life overseas and a desire to join those who had now demonstrated that it was a viable move, were being communicated through letters home from those already settled.

The climate of North Carolina would have been congenial for growing crops, but it also encouraged a vegetation cover of trees. For the settlers, the circumstances of their chosen new environment placed them in the position of pioneers, faced with the daunting task of virgin forest clearance. On the other hand, land was so plentiful that they could afford to engage in something resembling the shifting cultivation of the Amazon Forest Indians, where land is farmed, depleted of its soil fertility, then abandoned as a fresh tract is prepared for crop growing.

This and other colonial settlements in North America were, however, only a prelude to the population movements to come. Famine conditions at home, following the disastrous crop yields of the early years of the 1780s, became another powerful push factor resulting in a further boost to emigration, and the exodus from mainland Highland parishes in particular was now speeding up. It is important to note, however, that at this stage emigration was not related to pressures from landowners to move away. On the contrary, there appears to have been widespread concern at the scale of the outward flow, and at the worrying loss of money both out of the local economy and from the country as a whole as the people sold up their stock and possessions to realise capital for their new lives overseas.

But now the focus of interest for new settlement was set to change from America to Canada. In the 1760s and early 1770s, Scots emigrants had begun to trickle into the continent's north-east corner, to Prince Edward Island and Nova Scotia. Availability of a substantial amount of land for reclamation at Pictou in Nova Scotia drew settlers from Inverness-shire, Sutherland and Ross-shire. The events surrounding this early settlement figure strongly in the annals and folk tradition of this part of Canada and have been interestingly portrayed, for example, in Donald MacKay's book *Scotland Farewell* which concerns itself with the 200 people on the *Hector*, a 'leaky old brig' which sailed from Loch Broom in Wester Ross to Pictou in 1773. There is no doubt that for the people who chose to uproot themselves from their native parts, the new provinces were something of a promised land. The problem was that getting there involved an unpleasant ocean voyage in frequently harsh and cramped conditions, and the death toll from disease was frequently high.

Soon reports on the advantages of life in the Maritime Provinces were reaching receptive ears back home. This acted as an encouragement to others, and the movement started to gather momentum. Significantly, the landscape and general environmental conditions of the area were not dissimilar to those left behind, so that the trauma of resettlement was at least cushioned by being in an environment that was not disturbingly different from home. The emigrants also derived some security from leadership, whether by tacksmen or clergymen. Another significant factor was that large numbers from the same communities emigrated together, giving a strong sense of corporate identity within the new communities which long remained a feature of life in these places and ensured a lasting 'Scottishness' of outlook and personality.

Nova Scotia's maritime neighbour, Prince Edward Island, was the focus of settlement for hundreds of emigrants from the

Gaelic chapel, Cromarty in the Black Isle. Here the workers attracted by the town's 'mini' Industrial Revolution could worship in their own tongue.

west coast and Hebrides. The prime mover in this emigration was Lord Selkirk who also attempted to establish a settlement in upper Canada. Much further to the west, in Canada's continental heartland, Selkirk acquired land in the early part of the 19th century. This, his Red River settlement, attracted emigrants from the Highlands and Orkney. Indeed, for a time this Manitoban settlement was very much dominated by Orkneymen, until a great wave of new settlers in the latter part of the century diluted its strong Orcadian character.

When it is recalled that the lairds of the time depended totally on a large labour force to produce the kelp that provided their incomes, it is hardly surprising that Selkirk's encouragement of emigration should have been viewed in such a poor light at home. Alarmed by this steady erosion of the kelping workforce, the lairds were determined to press their objections to it at the highest levels. Government response to the problem was first to commission a survey that linked the subject of communications in the north and west with the means of reducing the now widespread emigration. Thomas Telford was the civil engineer appointed to the task, and his later work with roads, bridges, harbours and the Caledonian Canal, was greatly to improve the communications infrastructure of the area.

The Passenger Vessels Act was passed in 1803. It acknowledged the stress and suffering which had resulted from the unregulated carrying of emigrants across the Atlantic in the previous decades, and proposed a series of measures to reduce the number of passengers who could be legally carried, as well as introducing regulations governing the quality of life on board ship. Considering the notorious conditions of past voyages, the act was without doubt a way of ensuring an improvement in the situation. But, at the same time, it had the inevitable effect of raising the cost of passage, for the new measures would have to be paid for by those who organised the voyages.

The truth was, of course, that implied in the new arrangements was the plan that numbers crossing the Atlantic would drastically reduce, for those who had been making the passage had invariably managed to scrape just enough together to pay for their travel. The landowners could well take satisfaction in the government's action, for it answered the fear that mass depopulation would drain their estates of their all-important work forces.

That the landowners' attitude was set to change so soon and so fundamentally is a measure of how much the humanitarian interest really was worth when weighed against selfish economic considerations. By the 1820s, sheep farming was displacing people from the highland straths and other inland situations. Giant sheep walks were becoming the order of the day and the old farming townships stood in the way of that perceived form of progress. At the same time, the kelp industry had undergone its mammoth collapse as supplies of cheap foreign substitute flooded the home market. The same lairds who had held up their hands in horror at the very thought of overseas emigrations now looked upon it as an answer to the problem of what to do with the people who were congesting the islands and the mainland's coastal edge. Previously, hundreds of crofters had petitioned their landowners for help with emigration, so that the image of the landowning tyrant forcing a peasantry from their native shores is not entirely correct. But while the lairds may not have directly forced their tenants' removal, their part in the circumstances that led to the conditions which drove the people to seek emigration should not be forgotten.

In this changed perception of the situation, many were now given financial encouragement by the lairds to seek a new life elsewhere. In this way, for example, MacLean of Coll emptied an island of its population, for, apart from one family, all 300 and more residents of the Inner Hebridean island of Rum were given financial assistance to sail to a new life in Canada. Where island folk once cultivated their rigs and tended their cattle, sheep were put in to convert the grazings into a highly profitable wool clip, and later owners, like Sir George Bullough in his magnificent castle, lorded it over an empty island.

Other lairds were reluctant to see their people depart, though this attitude became untenable when food supplies were threatened by the potato famine. In the 1840s and 1850s, thousands of emigrants left the crofting province, bound for Canada. Between 1851 and 1855, Lewis alone is said to have lost a staggering 14% of the entire island population. There, the Matheson estate pursued draconian measures to identify suitable candidates for emigration. Rent arrears were considered a justification for removal, and several townships lost their entire populations through eviction.

While the exact circumstances surrounding emigration varied from place to place, it is clear that in many cases removal of substantial numbers of people was not followed by any real improvement in the lot of those who were left. The clearance exercise should have functioned as something of a safety valve, removing the pressure of overpopulation among the congested districts of the crofting areas. Rather than arrange for some redistribution of land to overcome the problems of small scale landholding which excessive subdivision had created, however, ruthless estate proprietors merely pressed on with the business of creating ever more sheep grazings.

Colonel Gordon of Cluny held an Aberdeenshire estate title, but was also owner of the south Hebridean islands of Barra, South Uist and Benbecula. Around 1851, several hundred islanders from Gordon's estate emigrated to Canada. Reluctant though they may have been to look upon their native island for the last time, they can have shed few tears for severing their links with a landlord who had shown such lack of feeling towards his tenants during the hungry years. Their destitute condition was even a cause for concern by the Quebec immigration officials handling their entry into Canada.

A little further to the north of Gordon's Hebridean estate, were the MacDonald lands on the island of North Uist. But though the ownership might be different, the circumstances were much the same. Immigration officials in Quebec in 1849 again commented unfavourably upon the condition of over 200 arriving North Uist settlers. Other new settlers had had the dignity of clothing, food and means of travel when they arrived. The North Uist people were so destitute that they required considerable charitable help on their arrival in Ontario.

Not unnaturally, such circumstances were the subject of interest outwith the Highlands, and did not escape the notice of contemporary social commentators like Hugh Miller of the Edinburgh newspaper, *The Witness*. It would be quite wrong, however, to assume that the people meekly accepted the landowners' dictates as far as emigration was concerned, though individual resistance was swiftly disposed of. At the Napier Commission hearing at Breasclete, a delegate recounted the facts as they were remembered in the township long after the event:

'One of the men who was sent . . . to Lochganvich, and afterwards was sent to America, was unwilling to emigrate. The officers came to his house and quenched his fires, and sent him out of the house to the steamer that was waiting to carry him away, and his only cow was left at the back of the door, and he got nothing for it. His brother afterwards sold the cow, and sent the proceeds to him.'

In the summer of 1849, trouble had flared up at Sollas in North Uist when an attempt was made to evict the crofters who refused to comply with the estate's plans for their future. Needless to say, this involved their clearance from the land and removal to Canada, a familiar remedy for difficulties whose seeds had been sown in the palmy days of the kelp industry by deliberately encouraging population growth and croft sub-division. No doubt the estate officials considered that their offer of a free passage and cancellation of all rent arrears was a

Kinloch Castle, Rum. The later lairds of this Inner Hebridean isle lorded it over a lonely place, for clearance had emptied it of its people.

generous one, but the people of the Sollas district considered otherwise.

Again, media interest has ensured the survival of a record of the events at Sollas, the *Inverness Courier* having sent its reporter west to cover the newsworthy events. When a squad of 30 men from the Inverness-shire constabulary descended upon the district on a July day in 1849, they proceeded with their task of forced removal by destruction of roofs and personal effects. A large group of local people had converged on the scene, intent on resisting the evictions of kinsfolk and neighbours. Stones began to fly, and it became clear that the squad had a major resistance on its hands. The following day served only to heighten the tension, the trauma of the occasion resulting in scenes of hysteria, and the women turning upon the police with a volley of stones. Now the people were given the choice of being evicted there and then, or signing a pledge that they would remove themselves in the spring of the following year. In effect, the end result was that the estate was able to have its way with its clearance policy, and the Sollas crofters had little option but to join the emigrant stream.

The MacDonald lands in Skye fared little better, with widespread removals from the coastal townships. One of the best known eye-witness descriptions of emigrants' departure is recorded in the words of Sir Archibald Geikie, the celebrated Scots geologist and writer. Geikie was witness in 1853 to the highly emotive departure of Skye folk after their enforced removal from the townships of Suishnish and Boreraig on the MacDonald estate.

'. . . One afternoon, as I was returning from my ramble, a strange wailing sound reached my ears at intervals on the breeze from the west. On gaining the top of one of the hills on the south side of the valley, I could see a long and motley procession winding along the road that led north from Suishnish. It halted at the point of the road opposite Kilbride, and there the lamentation became loud and long. As I drew nearer, I could see that the minister and his wife and daughters had come out to meet the people and bid them all farewell. It was a miscellaneous gathering of at least three generations of crofters. There were old men and women, too feeble to walk, who were placed in carts; the younger members of the community on foot were carrying their bundles of clothes and household effects, while the children, with looks of alarm, walked alongside. Everyone was in tears. . . . When they set forth once more, a cry of grief went up to heaven, the long plaintive wail, like a funeral coronach, was resumed, and after the last of the emigrants had disappeared behind the hill, the sound seemed to re-echo through the whole wide valley of Strath in one prolonged note of desolation. The people were on their way to be shipped to Canada. I have often wandered since then over the solitary ground of Suishnish. Not a soul is to be seen there now. . . .'

In 1851, the Government passed the Emigration Advances Act which empowered landowners to borrow from public funds

Crumbling ruins bear silent testimony to the exodus from the land which has characterised the crofting province.

the necessary capital to assist the removal of their tenants by emigration. By 1852 the Highlands and Islands Emigration Society was organising a controlled emigration from parishes the length and breadth of the Hebrides and Highland mainland. Several thousand people left under the auspices of the Society, with a considerable number of these from the MacDonald lands on Skye, representing the poorest in the island: the cottars and the landless. Some of those who left the islands at this time lacked even the decency of proper clothes, and had to be furnished with clothing before departing. Those charged with managing the exodus must have stared many times upon the stark face of destitution as the emigrant stream filed slowly past.

But it was not only to destinations in the northern hemisphere that the emigrants went. Coinciding with the bad crop years of the 1830s came a new outlet for Highland folk as free and subsidised passages became available to Australia, hitherto the destination of those condemned to transportation by the courts. Now the emerging Australian stock-rearing economy was in need of a substantial work force, the more so since the great gold rushes to Ballarat and Bendigo had drained the peripheral settlement areas of much of their own labour supply. The overcrowded population of the crofting province, made redundant, in fact, by precisely the same kind of collapse of demand for labour that characterised many gold-digging areas, could supply that need in part at least.

By the 1850s the exodus to the Antipodes had greatly increased, aided by the work of the Highland and Island Emigration Society. In a few years following its establishment, the Society had assisted many hundreds to leave for Australia with the cooperation of the Colonial Land and Emigration Commission who arranged passages. For a time, in the early 1850s, Australia could rival Canada in its pull on those who sought a new beginning. By the decade's end, however, there was a recovery in farming and a growing demand for labour from the industrial central lowlands which reduced the flow to Australia. The much shorter length of journey to Canada also acted as a greater pull.

The transatlantic voyage was bad enough at the best of times, but the much more lengthy passage to Australia was a greater trial by far. The *Hercules* which sailed for South Australia in 1852 carried emigrants from Skye, Harris and South Uist. After enduring severe storm conditions, many of the passengers and crew were struck down by typhus and smallpox, the scourge of the emigrant ships. For a time the ill-fated vessel remained at Cork in southern Ireland before resuming her voyage with a greatly depleted passenger list. Some had died, some resumed their journey on other ships, and some, tragically, returned as orphans to the homes from which they had set out with parents buoyed up by the hope of better family times ahead.

One famous group of emigrants from Assynt in the north-west mainland reached Australia after having settled in Canada first. Their leader, Norman MacLeod, a Presbyterian who held no truck with the Church of Scotland, sailed to Pictou in Nova Scotia in 1817, and was joined soon afterwards by a substantial group of followers from Assynt. Encouraged by reports of life in Australia, MacLeod led his group to settle there in 1851, when the country was gripped by the fever of the gold rushes. Disenchanted with the conditions of the place, MacLeod and his people then set sail for New Zealand where they established their community on the Waipu River in 1853.

The agencies which assisted in the mass movements of people from the crofting lands of the Highlands and Islands to Canada and Australia have been accused of collaborating in the enforced removal of thousands of people. Though their reasons for assisting the passage of the people may have been based on humanitarian ideals, they were certainly of major help to the landowners in effecting the mass removal of what was perceived to be a redundant population. Sadly, the general impact on overcrowding of the coastal strips and overpopulation of the crofting community was decidedly limited. For those who were left behind, the grinding poverty of subsisting on hopelessly subdivided landholdings in a setting of congested crofting districts continued as before.

CHAPTER 7

The Crofters' War

In any consideration of the crofting story, the Crofters' War of a century ago marks a watershed in the thinking and behaviour patterns of the ordinary folk. That the word 'war' came to be used at all to refer to the succession of incidents which occurred is in itself a measure of the strength of unrest which had come to affect the crofting situation.

The fact was that the seeds of discontent and eventual conflict had been sown in those earlier troubled times through which the folk of the crofting townships had suffered long and in silence. Eviction and emigration, hunger and high-handed landlordism all played their part in the crofting saga. And now the memory and experience of them were to fuel the unrest and protest which would replace the old meekness with a new militancy, and send shudders through distant corridors of power. The memory of those militant times has not easily faded, and in recent times writers like I. M. M. MacPhail have written expressively of the events of the Crofters' War.

After the trauma of overcrowding, eviction and starvation, the crofters were now finding some vociferous supporters outwith their own ranks. Chief among those who put pen to paper to champion the crofters' cause was the radical figure of John Murdoch, founder of *The Highlander* newspaper in Inverness in 1873. In its columns he was not slow to air the sensitive issue of land reform, so that in Murdoch (and some others, too) a voice of questioning and protest was beginning to reach the ears of a widening and receptive audience.

In the following year, an event that might first have been considered a minor local difficulty grew into a subject attracting considerable outside interest, and now the means existed for bringing it to a wider public. The geographical setting was the island of Great Bernera off the west side of Lewis, whose crofters had traditionally moved their cattle to summer grazings on the other side of Loch Roag which separates the island from Lewis itself. In doing so, they were taking part in a time-honoured practice, shifting their cattle to the summer shielings that lay on hill ground several miles away, across on Lewis. This transhumance was an old established tradition, but tradition was to prove to be no guarantee of continuation, as the crofters were to find out.

As a result of the formation of sporting deer forest, the crofters of Bernera were given notice that they were to accept new grazings. These had perhaps some advantage of location, being much closer to their island, but had also the distinct disadvantage of being located on land which the crofters considered of inferior worth. It was agreed, however, that they should take the new land, and they proceeded to build a dyke, marking the line of division between grazings and deer forest. The dyke was not long constructed, however, when they were given notice to quit their new grazings and to summer their cattle on yet another area of land, this time on the island itself. Again, there was dissatisfaction over the nature of this latest area of grazings, not to mention the ill-feeling at having built, with considerable effort, the demarcating dyke.

Protest only brought the predictable summons of removal from Stornoway and these were duly served on the families. However, the enforcement officers whose duty it was to perform this mission left with more than their duty done in delivering the summonses, taking the road back to Stornoway with the angry protests of the Bernera folk still buzzing in their ears. And worse; the sheriff officer had lost patience with the taunts of some of the township children and committed an unfortunate indiscretion by threatening them.

By this time, the feelings of the township folk were inevitably running very high and found an outlet in an encounter with the sheriff officer which resulted in charges of assault being laid against three of the Bernera men. Their eventual acquittal, and the islanders' retention of their grazings became a pointer to the direction in which the politics of crofting were set to go.

In 1879, unrest came also to the mainland parish of Lochbroom in Wester Ross. The estate of Leckmelm which flanks the sea inlet of Loch Broom on its east side was bought by a Mr Pirie, a well-to-do paper mill proprietor from Aberdeenshire. Pirie's vision for his new purchase was of a profitable west coast estate run by paid workers. To achieve this end, he gave his tenantry the option of disposing of their stock at valuation worth and becoming his estate work force, or being evicted from the crofts which marked the slopes above the lochside.

In an age when improvements in communication and the beginnings of media attention were creating a less remote crofting province both in a physical sense and in the perception of the country as a whole, the affair attracted some outside interest. At the same time, the Highland societies were also helping to influence public opinion. Thus the *Ross-shire Journal* of November 26th, 1880, could report that at a meeting of 'Highlanders resident in London' a resolution was proposed 'That this meeting of London Highlanders expresses its deepest sympathy with the oppressed people of Leckmelm'.

Though the troubles in Lewis and Wester Ross had been significant events in themselves, they had only been part of the process leading inexorably on to the most dramatic events of the Crofters' War. It was on the northwards-pointing peninsula of Kilmuir on Skye that crofter agitation was next to flare up in a newsworthy fashion. Following a revaluation of land on the estate, a doubling of rents had been proposed for the November 1877 payment. The threat of removal from the land was sufficient at first to ensure that the rents were forthcoming, but three years later, Norman Stewart, a crofter from the township of Valtos, led a protest against the rent rises.

Refusal to pay the increased rents by the tenants of Valtos and the neighbouring township of Elishader at the due collection date was followed by the predictable threat of eviction from the landlord. The eventual reduction of the two township rents by a quarter was enough to guarantee peace in the short term but insufficient to avert the unrest which was to follow in other parts of Skye.

The district known as the Braes lies between six and eight miles to the south of Portree, Skye's main settlement. The crofters who worked its township lands had the knowledge of the rent strike of the Valtos and Elishader crofters behind them as they now entered the fray in what is remembered as one of the most significant events of the Crofters' War. Once more, at the heart of the issue was the matter of common grazings, encapsulating all the crofters' grievances concerning the shortage of land. The slopes of Ben Lee, high above Loch Sligachan, had

Now linked to Lewis by bridge across Loch Roag, the distant island of Great Bernera figured early on in the Crofters' War.

long been used as a common grazing by the crofters of the townships which face across the Sound of Raasay. The grazings had, in fact, been lost to the crofters a number of years earlier, but their grievance over the matter had not gone away, and now it was to come to the surface again.

The crofters, quite simply, were refusing to pay their rents to the MacDonald estate. To understand more of the background to this dispute, it is important to set Braes into the context of land agitation in other parts of the Atlantic edge. Throughout the west of Ireland, the same kind of folk had been made to thole the same kind of privation and oppression. They had shared the same pangs of hunger in the terrible times of the Potato Famine, though in an even more serious way, and had suffered similar treatment from some landlords and their factors.

The Irish Land League with Charles Stewart Parnell as its president had been founded in 1879 against a background of evictions on a massive scale. Parnell it was who introduced the practice of 'boycotting', at once effectively pressing his political point and giving the English language a new word. The passing by Parliament of the Irish Land Act, giving in to many of the League's demands such as security of tenure and legally determined rents, was an achievement for those who had actively worked for the cause of the long-oppressed in rural Ireland. It also proved to be an encouragement and incitement to some of the crofters of Skye.

The prelude to trouble at the Braes was the familiar progress of the sheriff's officer, sallying forth from Portree with a pocketful of summonses of removal for some of the tenants who had withheld their rent. Though the law might have been on the landlord's side, the crofters' feelings certainly were not. At the officer's approach, a crowd gathered and closed in upon him. The eviction papers were put into a heap and defiantly set on fire.

The action of the Braes crofters must have set the alarm bells ringing in Portree. By assaulting the sheriff's officer, the crofters were guilty of the crime of deforcement, and that was a serious matter. Being part of the county of Inverness, the Braes incident was one for the Inverness-shire police force, but the scale of the reprisal envisaged by Sheriff William Ivory demanded a far greater number of men. This deficiency was quickly overcome, however, by the deployment of a force from the Glasgow Constabulary, making the Sheriff's force around 50 strong.

Having arrived at Portree on the MacBrayne steamer, *Clansman*, the police squad was marched, on a miserable day of pouring rain, the six or so miles to the nearest township of Gedintailor. These first crofters of the Braes were still abed under their thatched roofs and certainly not expecting such an unwelcome visitation at that early hour of the morning. At the township of Balmeanach, things were to turn out differently, and the police action in arresting the men on the deforcement charge brought a hostile crowd together. In a few minutes, battle had been well and truly joined and the 'Battle of the Braes' was to go down in the annals of crofting history as a high point in the struggle for crofters' rights.

With sticks and stones being rained upon their heads, the police were able to withdraw with their captives only after making a strong baton charge. Several of the Braes women were left cut and bleeding. By succeeding in having the arrested men marched back to the jail in Portree, Sheriff Ivory and his police squad had arguably won the battle, but the war would carry on. And worse from the landlords' point of view was the presence of a somewhat different squad, one now preparing to go to Skye and ready to report back to their newspaper offices on the crofter troubles.

At the trial of the Braes men in Inverness Sheriff Court in May, 1882, the charge of deforcement was withdrawn and the accused given fairly lenient fines. The trial had shown up the factor in a rather poor light and could in no way be seen as any kind of success for the landowner. Instead, the crofters could claim their own moral victory. But trouble was not yet to pass by the Braes. The township livestock, whether by accident or design, were now wandering freely over the grazings of Ben Lee, the original focus of the crofters' discontent.

A messenger at arms, dispatched from Portree with a Court of Session summons, got short shrift when he attempted to enter the Braes townships. With so many of their men away at sea, it was left to the women, now practised in the art of propelling clods at the unwelcome representatives of the law, to drive the bearer of the summons back to Portree. Their actions, however, were held once more to constitute deforcement, and repercussions were bound to follow.

Faced with such a strength of crofter protest, Sheriff Ivory requested that the Government provide military assistance to the upholders of the law on Skye by sending in 100 troops. His request was not looked upon with any favour, but instead met by a suggestion that the Inverness-shire police force be considerably increased to cope with any unrest of the recent type.

After a further confrontation between the police and the people of the Braes in October, 1882, a settlement of the thorny issue of Ben Lee was arrived at. The representatives of Lord MacDonald were prepared to concede a reduction in the rent for the Ben Lee grazings. The rent strike was at an end. After all the strife, peace had arrived on the Braes, but the troubles in Skye were set to continue for some time to come.

The underlying crofter grievance of land shortage was now finding expression in a variety of different situations. To the west of Dunvegan with its ancient seat of the MacLeods, lie the lands of Glendale. There the crofters of several townships, starved of grazing land for their stock, had also been staging a rent strike. Now they were casting their eyes on the sheep farm of Waterstein whose tenant did not intend to renew his lease.

Already angered by the petty dealings of the estate factor, the crofters of Glendale were in no mood to accept that the Waterstein grazings over which their ancestors' stock had roamed should now pass into the hands of this very man for whom they had such little liking. Resentment at the removal of the crofters' cattle from the Waterstein grazing resulted in a confrontation with the shepherds in which one of them suffered an assault. Like the crofters of Braes, and fortified by a feeling of right on their part, the folk of Glendale awaited the challenge of the law from their township fastness.

That challenge was to come the following spring when a group of policemen was sent in from Dunvegan. Battle was soon joined with the Glendale crofters, but it was an uneven match, and the officers of the law were only too relieved to escape back to Dunvegan whence they had come. Next day, a messenger of arms, intent on serving notices of interdict, as well as over a dozen policemen, had to make a strategic withdrawal when confronted by an angry crowd of crofters.

A gunboat was now dispatched with a civil servant on board whose remit was to try to persuade five wanted Glendale men to submit to the authority of the law. After a well-attended meeting at Glendale Free Church, this they did and were duly sent off the island. The Glendale five were found guilty and given jail sentences at the Court of Session in Edinburgh. Needless to say, their return to the townships two months later was a cause for celebration on a grand scale. The men who had gone off to jail in Edinburgh had come back in triumph as martyrs to the crofters' cause.

In the spring of 1883, the Government announced its intention to set up a Royal Commission 'to inquire into the condition of the Crofters and Cottars in the Highlands and Islands of Scotland'. With some uncertainty over the likely effectiveness of this move, and following the example of the Irish Land League, some of crofting's most staunch supporters in the south set up the Highland Law Land Reform Association.

Memorial cairn at the Braes, Isle of Skye.
Here, under the shadow of Ben Lee, crofters of the Braes achieved lasting fame
for their defiant stand against perceived injustice.

Not long afterwards, on May 8th, the Napier Commission, bearing the name of its lordly chairman, opened its very first hearing into crofters' grievances — at Ollach Schoolhouse at Braes.

It was not until 1886, two years after the publication of the Napier Commission Report, that the Crofters' Holding Bill passed through Parliament. In the intervening period the crofting movement had come to assume a high profile outside and to be marked by widespread agitation on its home front. Rent strikes and occupations of grazings were rife throughout mainland and island parishes, and trouble had returned again to Skye.

Perhaps separation from home while at the summer fishing had strengthened the Skye men's resolve, but whatever the reason, trouble flared up at Kilmuir. Deep-seated dissatisfaction found a focus in the unpopular estate factor. Worried that the Kilmuir crofters were apparently beyond the law in their dealings with both the estate and all officialdom, the authorities were now to sanction the carrying of revolvers by the police in Skye. And at last, Sheriff Ivory was to have his long-denied wish come true; the Government was at last prepared to dispatch troops to deal with the militants in the Misty Isle.

Gunboat diplomacy — or certainly gunboat deployment — manifested itself in November with the appearance of a small fleet, consisting of a shipful of marines with gunboat escort and an attending MacBrayne's steamer, the *Lochiel*, with the Sheriff on board. It must have been an impressive sight for the crofters in the townships along the island edge who watched the flotilla's progress, sailing round to Uig Bay. But the nature of what the whole affair was about was soon to be questioned by many who were far from that island shore that winter day.

Once arrived at Uig, the force of more than 300 marines was marched, in an outwardly impressive show of strength, on through the crofting townships. No doubt the newspaper correspondents were hoping that lawlessness would manifest itself and thus guarantee them a good story. But the crofters presented an entirely passive picture as they viewed the expedition's progress and went about their daily chores. By the beginning of December the greater part of the force of marines withdrew from the island, leaving the remainder as a continuing military presence for a good six months later.

With such a show of strength to back them, the police had succeeded in asserting their authority in the many parts of Skye where it had been flouted and rejected for so long. The familiar landlord and factor complaint about rent strikes, however, was quite another matter.

Strong voices were being raised in support of the crofters' cause by a variety of outside speakers. The Highland Land Law Reform Association provided financial support for John MacPherson, the 'Glendale Martyr' to travel through the townships addressing receptive crofter meetings. Gifted with an eloquence of oratory and force of delivery, MacPherson stands out as one of the personalities during the time of the Crofters' War. Addressing his audiences in Gaelic, he would begin with prayer and reference would be made to Old Testament texts.

In an interesting paper in the *Scottish Geographical Magazine*, Donald E. Meek has explored the question of the land issue and the development of a Highland theology of liberation. The membership card of the Highland Land Law Reform Association, for example, bore the Ecclesiastes' text: 'The profit of the earth is for all'. In addition, it proclaimed the Gaelic motto of the Association: *Is treise tuath na tighearna*, meaning 'A tenantry is mightier than a laird'.

In fact, the Old Testament books abounded in texts which many saw to be apposite to the crofters' situation, not least the Book of Psalms' verse: 'The earth is the Lord's, and the fulness thereof', and the warning of Isaiah: 'Woe unto them that join house to house, that lay field to field, till there be no place, that they may be placed in the midst of the earth'.

Among a god-fearing folk, it was no cause for surprise that familiarity with scripture would allow the crofters to identify with the oppressed in times gone by. Some ministers, notably of the Free Church, were also prepared to stand and be counted for the crofters' cause and preached what they felt should be practised by those who owned and managed the land. The Rev. Donald MacCallum was one of the few ministers of the established church to promote the crofters' cause. His ministry had taken him via Tiree and Lewis to Skye where he had cause to become familiar with the interior of the Portree jail. Some measure of the impact of his preaching may be sensed in the words of Mairi Mhor nan Oran, the Skye poetess, who wrote after hearing him: 'We saw the dawn break, and the clouds of thralldom flee away, the day MacCallum stood beside us at the Fairy Bridge'. Even in translation from the Gaelic, the sense of vision of liberation in a new dawn is powerfully conveyed.

Thus the liberation theology formed its own strand in the story of the Crofters' War. The dramatic show of strength in the Skye expedition in no way signalled the end to the crofters' disputes. Trouble flared up in townships throughout the west from Tiree in the Inner Hebrides across to the outer isles, and from Lewis down to South Uist. In 1886, aggrieved crofting tenants of the Duke of Argyll in Tiree were confronted by a force of policemen dispatched from the mainland. When this failed to subdue them, two warships with a large complement of marines were sent in, while Skye saw yet another military expedition.

The problem of the cottars who often possessed only meagre

patches of potato ground reared its head. In November, 1887, a large group of squatter cottars entered the deer forest of Pairc in the parish of Lochs in Lewis. Land hunger and desperation for food for their families was said to have led the men to shoot a number of red deer. By now, the gunboats were well used to nosing their way in among the islands of the west, and in they came once more. In January, 1888, battle was joined between the land-hungry crofters and the military at Aignish on the Point Peninsula beyond Stornoway.

The Crofters' War had demonstrated the depth of feeling of the crofters and the lengths to which land hunger was prepared to drive them. In a subsistence economy, many crofter folk who lived in the townships (not to mention the hard-pressed cottars) must have felt that they did not have much to lose. With so little wealth in material terms, the legacy of resentment handed down from generation to generation from the days of the mass evictions was bound to influence the thinking and aspirations of the crofters. While the days of the Luddites and Tolpuddle Martyrs are familiar to many in Scotland from school history lessons, the story of the often fiery days of the Crofters' War against landlords and legality deserves to be better known.

This was not, however, to be the end of unrest in the crofting areas. The related problems of high density of population and insufficient land to support it found expression in further incidents of land raiding. At government level the response was to establish in 1897 a Congested Districts Board, largely based on the Irish model. The areas of the Board's attention were those places where the difficult socio-economic conditions were creating the greatest pressures, but this was later extended to include most of the crofting locality. Under the aegis of the Board, considerable improvements were made to the communications infrastructure of the region through road and pier construction. Land improvements through drainage were backed by the promotion of better farming methods and more selective breeding of livestock. Crofters' shows were actively encouraged, providing a spirit of competition to help foster livestock improvement.

One of the most celebrated examples of land raiding focused on the island of Vatersay. The problem of cottars had always

Landscape with crofts, Glendale. From here, the Glendale Martyrs left for imprisonment in Edinburgh for their support of the crofters' cause.

been a particular feature of the Hebrides. Gross overcrowding on Barra induced a number of cottars to attempt a settlement on the smaller island. After a protracted period of unrest and a series of attempts at establishing crofts on Vatersay, the Board was eventually able to acquire the island for the purposes of land settlement. In Lewis, cottar land raiding was to remain a feature of island life and politics into the 1920s, and the practice was to continue sporadically elsewhere.

In 1911, after a considerable contribution to the crofters' lot throughout the Highlands and Islands, the Congested Districts Board had been dissolved and its functions transferred to the new Board of Agriculture for Scotland. After the war years, the new Board built on the successes of its predecessor by creating hundreds of new crofter holdings. Through the Board's work, many of the most unpopular threads of past crofting history were unpicked. Pasture land was taken back from deer forest use and restored as common grazings. In Skye and elsewhere, large tracts of land were acquired and a pattern of smallholdings restored.

The birth of crofting was thus a protracted one, and the birth pangs often attended by considerable difficulty. To look upon the crofting scene today is to look upon a pattern of living that may seem deceptively simple in outward form. The reality is that it is the outcome of a decidedly complex chapter in Scottish history.

CHAPTER 8

The Napier Commission

As firmly as the year 1066 takes its place in English history, so 1886 stands out in the history of crofting in Scotland for it is the year in which crofting's most significant milestone was reached with the passing of the Crofters Holding Act. This followed in the wake of the Report of a Royal Commission in which crofting was put under a spotlight bright enough to illumine some dark closets and to bring the people's grievances to the attention of the nation.

The fact was that the land agitation and the lawlessness which attended it had so concerned the government that at last they were prepared to give some positive response to pressure for an official investigation into the true state of the lives and living of the crofters of Scotland. For the first time, the ordinary folk were actually to be encouraged to have their say, and all would be faithfully listened to, recorded and set out in the official government record which was to follow. Significantly, what they did say was said with an openness and noted down in an exactness that provides a unique commentary on life as it was lived by the ordinary crofting folk in those difficult times.

In March 1883, the Home Secretary, Lord Harcourt, had announced the setting up of a Royal Commission. In legalistic language its remit was 'to inquire into the conditions of the crofters and cottars in the Highlands and Islands of Scotland'. But in human terms it was to present an overdue opportunity for the crofters to give voice to the many grievances that had been felt for so long. It was with listening in mind that the Commission, chaired by Lord Napier of Ettrick, now set out to do its work.

At their disposal was the smart naval steam yacht, HMS *Lively*, which would take them in their journeying from Shetland in the north to Argyll in the south. Even remote St Kilda was to have its hearing, and by the time the Commissioners had completed their task they must have been well-seasoned travellers among the unpredictable waters of the voes, firths, sounds and sea lochs of the northern and western coasts. As it turned out, the handsome *Lively* was not to be their means of transport and floating accommodation for long, for after sailing to Skye, the Uists, Benbecula, Barra, St Kilda and the west of Lewis, she foundered ignominiously on the Chicken Rock just before reaching Stornoway. Fortunately, the Commissioners seemed to be little the worse for their experience, and were able to complete their work in Lewis and Harris before heading for the Northern Isles, but the vessel was unsalvageable.

There was a real appropriateness about the choice of the Commission's first place of hearing. The little school at Ollach in Skye was close to where the 'Battle of the Braes' had taken place such a short time before. Memories of the conflict were fresh in folk's minds, and the Glendale three were still within the confines of the Calton Jail in Edinburgh.

There must have been a sense of occasion on that May morning in 1883 when the Commissioners took their seats in the grey school building to listen to the delegates whom the crofters had chosen from their ranks. First to be examined was Angus Stewart, an articulate crofter from Braes. The high-handed estate factor, Alexander MacDonald, was less than happy that the crofters should be allowed such free expression of their feelings at all, and when asked by the Chairman if he wanted to make any comment was quick to add:

'I may say that I am surprised at this man's statement, because he is not one of our crofters at all. He is a crofter's son; he is not a crofter. That is the first thing. In the next place, I do not think that he has any reason whatever, if he tells the truth, and nothing but the truth, to fear anything. In fact, we consider it rather insulting to us to insinuate anything of the sort.'

To the crofters of the Braes, such an assurance was bound to have something of a hollow ring to it, and even the Chairman felt moved to question the worth of MacDonald's assurance. Stewart's reply both demonstrated his entitlement to speak on behalf of the crofters of the Braes and drew attention to the pettiness of the factor's comments. With the kind of down-to-earth eloquence which runs through so many of the crofter hearings, Stewart continued:

'I want to say a few words in English. It seems that Mr MacDonald objects to my evidence because I am only a crofter's son. My grandfather was born in Beinn-a-chorrain, and lived in Beinn-a-chorrain eighty-six years. He died there. My mother was born there, and is living there yet, at the age of eighty-four. I am forty years of age, and am living in Beinn-a-chorrain. I am married and have a family. I have been paying rent in Beinn-a-chorrain to Lord MacDonald for fifteen or sixteen years, and I think I have the right to bear evidence today'.

From the day of this very first hearing, the Commissioners can have been in no doubt about the feelings of the crofters and the deeply-felt nature of the grievances over land hunger and overcrowding which this first delegate went on to describe.

Stewart recalled for the Commissioners how the five tenants in Bein-a-chorrain in his grandfather's time had increased more than fivefold, the result of clearance off the deer forest land and of the population increase which was affecting the whole crofting area. In such circumstances there had been a clear need for more homes. But had the crofters been given any assistance in building them? Stewart's reply left them in no doubt:

'May the Lord look upon you! I have seen myself compelled to go to the deer forest to steal thatch — to steal the wherewith to thatch our houses. If we had not done so we should have had none; and I went in the daytime for this purpose, and was caught by the gamekeeper, and I had to give him part of what I had — part for the purpose of thatching his own house.'

When the Chairman asked Donald Buchanan, crofter of Lower Ollach, how long he had been in possession of his croft, his answer contained more than a hint of the crofters' perception of the omnipotence of the lairds and factors:

'I have been all my life on the croft which I now have, and I am now fifty-four years of age. I have seen the reigns of three Lords Macdonald in succession and seven factors.'

John Mathieson of Achnahannait who gave evidence was not a crofter, but a cottar with only a tiny plot of land. His evidence paints a picture of the constant subdividing of holdings which had reduced the crofting landscape to a patchwork pattern of hopelessly small pieces.

> 'I want to say that it is the want of land, and the dearness of it that is leaving the people so poor. My own great-grandfather was tenant in Achnahannait, and had a fourth part of it to himself. My grandfather succeeded him, and had a fifth part of Achnahannait. My father succeeded my grandfather, and had an eighth part of the land, and in his lifetime he came to be reduced to a sixteenth of the land. My father had six sons, of whom I am the eldest, and none of them would get a sod from Lord MacDonald.'

John McIntyre, crofter and missionary of Sconser described the ravages to the crofters' crops from marauding animals from the neighbouring deer forest which they just had to suffer, no matter how great the depredations. At Skeabost, the Commissioners listened to the evidence of William McClure, a crofter from Glen Bernisdale, who was also a fisherman and worked on the roads — a familiar combination. His evidence echoed that of the Braes hearings, but in one of those many passages which breathes real life into the Napier Report's tomes, he describes the crofters' delling instrument, not sparing the details of its deficiencies:

> 'As a proof that our holdings are too small, our only implement of agriculture is a stick with a crook at the end of it. We call it a caschrom, and if the stick has not a natural bend we have to nail a piece to it. Anyone capable of thinking must know that a man in two or three weeks cannot work sufficient ground with this implement to support a family of seven or eight.'

The situation of his township was one that had echoes throughout the whole crofting province: 24 families resettled on allotments of land taken away from the people of Bernisdale 47 years before.

The Commissioners heard how part of the township's hill ground had been taken away; how a yair (a kind of stone trap) in which the crofters caught herring had been destroyed because the landlord feared that it might catch some of his salmon as

Ollach, Skye, where the first hearing of the Napier Commission took place.

well; how seaweed had to be paid for if crofters wished to cart it from the shore to give some sustenance to their overworked land. Small wonder, then, that the ground was starved of feeding, as so many crofters were asserting.

That such detail and minutiae of everyday living were taken down and printed as minutes of evidence was a remarkable tribute to Victorian clerical exactitude, and forms an enduring record of the life and times of the people who walked to the hearings, at the invitation of a notice pinned on a local church door. In their evidence, though giving voice to a common sense of grievance, delegates from widely different locations each gave their individual testimony of life at the time, with all its privations and frustrations. They told of men and women, not beasts, dragging the harrows over the crop land; of crofters being refused permission to keep dogs and even horses, and of herdswomen abandoning the township cattle and fleeing home as the sportsmen's bullets flew over their heads. There are graphic comments on the quality of life (or frequently the lack of it), of insanitary living arrangements in crofter homes, and of the scourge of typhus among those who lived within them.

At Loch Boisdale in South Uist, Dr Black, a local medical practitioner, described the bronchial complaints suffered by the islanders in the spring, a pattern which he attributed to working out in the open with the caschrom while inadequately nourished – precisely the kind of situation which so often prevails in the developing world today where the productivity of peasant farmers is impaired by their diet-related poverty of health.

No doubt they would have been glad enough in the circumstances to secure a supply of *uisge beatha*. But whence did the people of Skye obtain their whisky, one of the Commissioners was keen to know. John Maclean of Waternish was able to furnish the information that supplies were obtained from the people of Gairloch in Wester Ross, 'and they were very kind people'. At this time, it might be added, the Gairloch 'smugglers' were noted both for their illicit stills out on the moors and for their success in outwitting the servants of Her Majesty who did their best to destroy them. Perhaps it was out of some concern for protecting the interests of the law-thwarting distillers of Gairloch that Maclean added:

'but it is a long time since we have seen any of them'.

At the Barra hearings, vivid accounts were given of the land hunger felt on the island, with descriptions of four crofters and nine cottars – 13 families in all – trying to eke a living from land where one crofter had worked the ground before. Farquhar McNeill of Bravaig described how seaweed to manure the potato patches was carried a distance of 12 miles in small boats, though the Commissioners were later to hear that the crofters of South Harris were forced to obtain their seaweed supplies from as far away as Skye.

Not only was seaweed a matter of crofter concern. Obtaining adequate supplies of peat could be equally problematical. John Mackay from South Uist gave voice to the complaint of cottars having been settled on his township's peat banks, and of those same people, out of sheer necessity, breaking in peat ground for crop growing in places which had previously served to provide the township's vital winter fuel.

Grievances over fuel supply were constantly aired. At

Breasclete, Murdo Macleod recounted how his township's peat banks had been taken from them altogether, and new ones allocated three miles away outside the township of Carloway.

'For half this distance there is no road, though we have to carry all our peats on our back. We have further to cross a river which, being without a bridge, is, after heavy rains, often dangerous and impassable. Our peats being so far away from us, and to relieve ourselves somewhat of the hardship of carrying the whole way on our backs, we sometimes have recourse to the expedient of floating them on the river for a certain distance, but as the river is let by the estate for fishing purposes, we are not allowed to float our peats on it till the beginning of January.'

Apart from the obvious difficulties of overcrowding, it is the sheer unsuitability of some of the land on which the crofters had been settled that emerges time and again. Perhaps nowhere is this more strikingly illustrated even today than in the rocky eastern edge of Harris. Roderick Ross graphically described the problems of living in such a harsh kind of land.

'It is all rocks. We are so surrounded by rocks that sometimes we never see the sun at all. There are three hours of the day when we don't know there is a sun at all.'

Donald Morrison, his neighbour, told the Chairman:

'Before my father's time there were no people there at all. No person can conceive what kind of place it is without seeing it. There is no highway there for cart nor horse.'

Morrison recalled the old system of land holding, with the arable ground reallocated each year. When asked whether that was better than the system of creating separate lots, he replied:

'The lots were better, but the people in these times preferred to have them in common. I have seen a woman weeping at being separated from her neighbours by the division of the crofts.'

On Saturday 2nd June, the ship bearing Lord Napier and the others anchored in Village Bay, St Kilda. Communication with St Kilda being what it was, the islanders were not expecting their visitors. As the Rev. John Mackay, Free Church minister, explained, his parishioners were less than enthusiastic about any outsider landing on their island shores. They had learned by bitter experience that visitors often left trouble behind them when they sailed, in the form of infectious diseases against which the isolated population had little or no immunity. Even the common cold could cause serious illness as it spread as an epidemic through the township.

At the Meavaig hearings in Lewis, John Mathieson, crofter and fisherman, told how crofters had broken in land at Aird Uig for the first time with no reward for all their labour.

> 'There are a few of the first crofters still living in the township, who have toiled all their lifetime taking in land and making improvements, and never got any compensation but their rents raised.'

It was becoming a familiar theme, as was the petty and sometimes brutish behaviour of some of the estate factors, and Mathieson could provide a local illustration:

> 'I will give one instance here of how factors treat some of their honest crofters. One of these first crofters, a very honest and respectable man who paid rents in the township for about fifty-five years, and was never one shilling in arrears all his lifetime, was about twelve years ago going to pay rent to the factor, a distance of thirteen miles, and being in his old age and getting frail, was a few minutes behind the rest of the crofters, and did not answer his name when called, was fined five shillings, and about thirty-five shillings put on his rent for having so much bad manners as to complain that it was not right to fine him under such circumstances.'

Malcolm Maclean of Swainbost told a similar story of displaced folk.

> 'The people asked the chamberlain at the time what he was then going to do with them when they had no homes, and he pointed to the sea, and told them their home was there.'

Yet those same oppressed families were giving up their young men into the service of the nation, John Macleod told the hearing at Tarbert.

The Napier Commission even ventured to remote St Kilda to hold one of its hearings. In this rock-girt place, sure-footed islanders harvested the seabirds and their eggs.

'There is not a family in the whole of Harris where there are two sons but one of them at least is in the service of the Queen, perhaps two, and neither they nor their fathers can obtain a foot of the soil upon which they could live. It would appear that when Britain becomes involved in a struggle with another nation in the future, they must send for the deer and the sheep of Harris as well as its young men, and then they can see which is the best bargain.'

In Shetland, the same grievances of lack of security of tenure, lack of compensation for improvements, removal of scattald or common grazings, overcrowding and sometimes eviction were voiced. John Omand, a crofter-fisherman of Mid Yell with three and a half acres of crop land stated his case quite simply:

'I would like some security so that I would get the good of my labour.'

In Baltasound in Unst, Thomas Abernethy was asked about the keeping of native Shetland sheep and the kind of return to be got from them. It appeared that seven shillings was the going price for a ewe and eight to nine shillings for a wether.

Thomas Ewanson from the island of Papa Stour told how the scattald had been fenced off from common use, yet rents were never reduced by way of compensation. The minister of the Free Church in Cunningsburgh had the same tale to tell, and could add that each crofter was also due the laird three days' labour per year and a kain hen for every merk of land held.

Lack of decent accommodation and pressure on what was available brought its own problems, as the minister testified.

'This overcrowding is inconvenient enough when a family is in health, but when there is sickness the state of things is simply heartbreaking.'

He instanced the case of a family struck down with typhoid. Distressed children and the lifeless corpses of those who had succumbed lay side by side as the disease brought the entire family down in their miserable and overcrowded one-apartment dwelling.

One of the most striking examples of high-handed landlordism was thrust into the limelight at the Orkney hearings in Kirkwall. Crofters from the hilly island of Rousay had elected as their spokesman the Reverend Archibald MacCallum. The list of grievances which he presented to the Commission was long, and hardly of an unfamiliar kind by now. But somehow, on reading these pages, the attitude of General Burroughs still sends a chill down the spine as his words ring out coldly from the past.

'Is the property mine, or is it not mine? If it is mine, surely I can do what I consider best for it? If these people are not contented and happy, they can go away.'

In the end, no assurance was to be forthcoming from the General that the crofters who gave evidence to the Commission would not suffer in consequence of it.

At the Bettyhill hearing on Sutherland's north coast, Adam Gunn, a crofter's son, described how in Strathy township there were now 42 crofters on land where, before the Sutherland clearances, there had been only four. Apart from the obvious problems of congestion, Gunn described the limitations of the coastal environment of townships like Leadnagullen to which the people had been cleared from the inland straths.

'We desire more arable land at a fair rent, and hill pasture, of which we may say we have none. We are unwilling to emigrate as long as there are so many depopulated glens in Sutherland-shire. The sea blast destroys our crops every other year, and we are thus compelled to carry meal for our families and provender for our cattle a distance sometimes of twenty miles. We do not want a tract of useless, barren, moorland, such as the neighbouring townships possess. Let us get a share of good hill pasture, and let an oversman appointed by Government fix the rent.'

When Angus Mackay, a crofter's son and divinity student from Farr, rose to his feet to speak on behalf of the crofters and cottars of his own and the neighbouring township, he was speaking on behalf of a people who had suffered in the notorious Sutherland clearances.

'The land our forefathers lived upon so happy and prosperous is now under deer and sheep, and turning into moss and fog, which is not profitable to man nor beast, while we are huddled together in small townships on the sea shore, exposed to all the fury of the wild sea breezes, which generally carry away the little corn we have. We want more land, security against eviction, compensation for improvements, and fair rent.'

That last sentence stands as a summary of so much of the feeling of an aggrieved people, vented so often at the dozens of hearings the length and breadth of the crofting province. Perhaps Angus Mackay spoke with more articulation than some of the other ordinary folk who had travelled by boat and on foot to have their say before the Commission. Yet the plain words spoken by the crofters so often stand out in surprising relief from the crowded pages of text in which they are set. In 1884 the lengthy Report of the Napier Commission was published. It was, without doubt, a watershed in the annals of crofting history, though the reaction to it was very mixed.

The outcome of this searching look at the social and economic circumstances of the crofting community was the first Crofting Act, giving statutory recognition to the rights of the people and establishing a Crofters Commission. By the time of its final report in 1912, the Commission had dealt with the accumulated problems of arrears of rent, security of tenure and compensation for improvements carried out by crofters.

A sequence of further legislation in the early part of the century was followed by the Taylor Commission into Crofting Conditions which reported in 1954. The Crofters (Scotland) Act of 1955 provided for the establishment of a new Commission, one which continues to deal with matters relating to crofting. The Crofters Reform (Scotland) Act of 1976 provided the right of a crofter to buy his or her own house as well as the inbye land around it, and many have done so.

For the factors who once ruled their masters' estates in such a high-handed fashion, the very idea would have been quite abhorrent. For today's crofters it was the last stage in the long struggle towards the right of security, a struggle which their ancestors had begun in the Crofters' War all those years ago.

CHAPTER 9

House and home

Issues of social and political history, such as the Clearances and the Crofters' War, have been the frequent subject of comment in the social history of crofting. The origins of the crofting system have also been much discussed and rightly so, for it is a significant part of Scotland's human story. And yet, the ways of crofter folk, the organisation of their lives and the day-to-day nature of their living are subjects worthy of interest for their own sake, for they speak volumes on life as it was conducted by those who sought their subsistence in the crofting province.

The circumstances of their lives were hard, sometimes subject to harsh unfairness, and frequently influenced by factors that were outwith their control. Viewed from today's perspective, amidst the excesses of an affluent society, we may judge that the crofter folk were poor, endowed with little in material terms. Yet what they did possess was an expression of a distinctive culture, something that was rich in a different kind of way. Ironically, out of the privations and poverty of the past have been bequeathed to our times an enduring impress on the land itself, a distinctive material culture, and a written record. Together they form a substantial part of Scotland's heritage.

In times past, books on Scotland were wont to include a photograph of a thatched cottage, with a caption such as 'The home of the crofter', as if portraying the habitat of some unusual species. After years of attempting to educate otherwise intelligent and rationally-thinking pupils in the north-east of Scotland in the geography of their native land, I used to be irritated to find some of them lapsing into writing about crofting in a way that suggested that the perception of a croft that exists in the general consciousness is still one of a small thatched house in some remote highland glen or on a windswept island. Somehow it is a perception that is difficult to shift. The reality is, of course, that there is far more to crofting than the house alone. Nevertheless, the traditional house types of the Highlands and Islands have much to tell us about the lives of the people who built and lived in them, and of their relationship to the land into which they had been set.

Even now, postcards showing thatched croft houses are still bought by holiday visitors to send home to their friends, though there is often little chance that they will have even glimpsed one on their travels. Such house types, with regional variant forms, were for long the traditional homes, but you will have to look hard to find an occupied one these days. Their demise has been quite rapid, and it is interesting to listen to the views of crofter folk on the matter. Many see in their passing the end of old days which were far from good in many senses. Others view their demise as the vanishing of yet another element of their cultural heritage, and with it a whole language of terminology to accompany it, for if there are no traditionally constructed buildings there is no longer a need for the many words and expressions that went with them.

Hugh Cheape has shown how an extraordinarily rich and varied selection of Gaelic terms surrounded the construction, mechanism and form of the little horizontal water mills in Lewis alone. Today, those mills have reality only in the memories of the older Leodhasachs, yet so much of the rich terminology which attended their construction and use has lingered on.

When houses of an improved, though still basic, type with slate or felt or even corrugated iron roofing came into being, they appeared bright by comparison with their old, low and dark-looking predecessors. They became known as *tigh geal* or white house, and therefore the older ones were described by the antonym *tigh dubh* or black house. It is no unusual thing these days to hear the term 'blackhouse' applied to just about any type of thatched house that survives in the Highlands, but the real blackhouse of the west was a most distinctive type of dwelling place.

Perhaps its most basic feature was the double wall construction which gave it a squat-looking appearance. The roof timbers rested on the inner wall, so that the rain ran down the thatch into the middle course of ground or sand. The result of the double thickness was not only a composite wall of extraordinary depth, but a means of insulating the occupants from wintry island blasts. The outer wall ledge or *tobtha* played its own part in the social life of the township, for it was a pleasant and

Number 42 Arnol, the best known croft house of all. Maintaining a building of this type into the future presents special problems. Here the blackhouse sports an incongruous polythene roof covering while renovations are carried out.

sheltered place on which to sit on fine summer days. Dr I. F. Grant reminds us that on South Uist the expression *Piobairean nan Tobhtaichean* (pipers of the tobtha) was applied to women who used the elevated ledge for calling in their menfolk, or for having a verbal set-to with other women of the township, for that matter. Being turfed over, the tobtha would sprout a bright summer growth of grasses and wild flowers that contrasted with the dark greyness of the building stone, and offered a tempting bite to an agile passing sheep.

In his *Letters from the Highlands* in the wake of the potato famine of 1846, Robert Somers has an interesting footnote on this distinctive feature.

'The people of Tiree turned the tops of their walls to a new use this last season. Those of them who were scarce of land sowed the garden-seeds sent them by the Ladies' Association round the roofs of their huts. I am told that the cottages, surmounted with rows of cabbages, have a very singular and grotesque appearance.'

Roofs in need of rethatching might also tempt an adventuresome beast if they sported a good growth of grass. If a beast with a head for heights was carrying any weight, trouble might ensue, as in one account which describes the discomfiture of the family at table inside at finding the legs of a cow suddenly pointing down at them through the thatch above.

Another prevailing idea seems to be that the blackhouse got its name from the fact that the interior was dark and sooty for want of a chimney, the peat reek from the central fire curling its way uncertainly upwards towards the thatch. Not surprisingly, the roof beams, turves and outer covering became thoroughly blackened, something that was a bit of a mixed blessing. On the one hand, the sooty deposit which impregnated the roof covering was the means of providing a source of organic fertiliser when the roof was replaced, as it frequently was on an annual basis. On the other, as John M. MacDonald wrote:

'The turf covering the rafters and under the thatch also got thoroughly saturated with peat smoke, and a black syrupy liquid formed in it and in damp weather dropped uncomfortably on the inmates of the house. When this happened, it was time for spring cleaning, which meant that the entire roof was removed, the rafters thoroughly scraped, and new layers of thatch and turf applied. The old turf and thatch removed from the roof made a most valuable manure when used along with sea-ware and farmyard manure, and the crofter was assured of a heavy crop of potatoes as a reward for his spring cleaning.'

When new crofts were being laid out by the estates last century, this annual replacement of the roof covering was being actively discouraged. Furthermore, efforts were being made to put an end to another tradition that stretched far back into time: the accommodation of both folk and livestock under the one roof with no internal wall separating them. Crofters always enjoyed a close relationship with the beasts with which they had constant contact, whether at milking time or when they were being moved on the tether to fresh grazing. They provided a most valuable contribution to the family diet in the form of milk and milk products, and they were, in many respects, the focus of family attention.

In addition to what the cows could produce by way of food, their warm breath doubtless helped raise the temperature on cold winter days and nights when the howling wind outside threatened to take the breath away. Many writers made much of the shared accommodation arrangements between man and beast, but in the matter of sharing the house with their animals, crofters were really no different from peasant farmers elsewhere. In the Alps, for example, mountain farmers slept in beds which were centrally heated from below by the rising warm breath of sheep housed inside a special compartment.

The best opportunity now to appreciate what the island black house was like is to pay a visit to Number 42 Arnol, 'held in trust for the nation by the Secretary of State for Scotland'. To supplement a visit there is a fine booklet by Professor A. Fenton who first visited the blackhouse in May 1964 when it was still occupied. He relates that his impression was of looking two ways in time, a feeling fostered by the contrasting sight of modern croft houses on the one hand, set alongside their blackhouse antecedents on the other.

At the time there were three generations living together in the blackhouse, all Gaelic speakers. The daily domestic chores of washing, cooking and preparing stock feed in the kitchen gave way to an evening by the peat fire and a chance to talk, tell stories, or attend to some task such as spinning or mending a creel.

When Alexander Fenton was travelling round the crofting areas in the 1960s, gathering so much valuable information on their material culture for the National Museum of Antiquities, I was engaged in my own researches in the historical geography of the Northern Isles. Our paths sometimes headed in similar directions, especially in those more out-of-the-way places which formed such a happy hunting ground for ethnographic enquiry. Like him, I shared that same feeling of being at a watershed in time, and that, sometimes poignant, awareness that here was a last glimpse of culture traits nearing their end, soon to pass from present reality into past history.

Today, many croft houses which were formerly thatched

have a roof covering of black tarred felt or rusting corrugated iron. The best place today to see the double-walled houses with thatched roofs of *muran* or bent grass is on the Uists or on the island of Tiree where they seem to spring with a freshness from the level green sward of the machair. Interest in the old houses is now high, in contrast to the situation not long ago when so many skilfully constructed dwellings tumbled into ruin without any thought of preserving them. In recent times, a largely island-based organisation called *Cairdean nan Taighean Tugha* (Friends of the Thatched Houses) has been instrumental in keeping alive the old roofing tradition and pressing for grants for their occupants not only on Tiree but elsewhere in the islands and on the mainland. Recently they supported the rethatching of a house in Wester Ross with a traditional covering of rushes.

In the Western Isles, the modern dwelling place often stands alongside the blackhouse which it displaced, allowing the visitor a last look at the expression of a way of living which looked to the land to supply most of its needs, something that does not happen today. What was remarkable about the old croft houses was how they seemed so much a part of the land in a way that their modern Department of Agriculture-approved successors are not. This is hardly surprising when it is remembered how much of the land actually did go into their construction. The stones and sods for walls were gathered from the ground, and the turves that covered the *cabairs* or roof timbers under the thatch were likewise stripped from the land round about. Sometimes the house was built into a slope, giving an even stronger impression of being an extension of the land. The thatch itself, whether of straw, bent, rush or heather, was obtained nearby. Straw or heather ropes kept it in place, and locally-gathered stones were employed to anchor it down against the gales.

Roofs were often supported on curving cruck beams set into the walls and tied at the top with wooden pins. Timber supply for the roof supports was a problem in a province where wood resources were often scarce, hence the preoccupation with beachcombing in coastal townships. Though in the story of *Whisky Galore*, Compton Mackenzie portrayed Hebridean islanders intent on mass removal of bottles of *uisge beatha* off

Houses in the Northern Isles were a rich expression of vernacular building traditions. Here roped thatch partly covers a North Ronaldsay flagstone roof.

the ill-fated cargo ship, the reality is that the gathering in of the sea's largesse has always been part and parcel of living along the Atlantic edge for crofting townships, though in a treeless island situation the washing ashore of a deck cargo of sawn timber might well be a cause for just as much rejoicing as the finding of a case of whisky. The Northern Isles minister who offered up a prayer that there might be no shipwrecks round his treacherous island shores did not forget to add the important rider that should some unfortunate calamity just happen to occur, he trusted that in his mercy the Good Lord would not forget the poor folk of his parish!

Thatching was a normal means of roof covering throughout the Northern Isles as well, the straw roof coverings being firmly roped down and secured with weighting stones. In Caithness and across the Pentland Firth, heavy flat flagstones were employed for roofing, sometimes even with thatch on top, and on Caithness crofts the same conveniently worked slabs were used for such diverse things as henhouses, animal troughs, field boundaries, gateposts and even clothes poles. Byre stalls were easily formed by setting a convenient piece of flagstone or schist on end, and a hole in the wall sometimes facilitated the removal of the dung to the outside.

In the longhouse tradition the byre dwelling, where human home and livestock housing were joined together, was a link with early times. Any degree of slope on the site usually dictated that the byre end be lower down for the practical purpose of drainage. Rounded stones from the beach could be set into the ground to form a firm floor for the livestock which passed the winter days in the dark interior of the byre. The preserved byre-dwelling at Laidhay in Caithness demonstrates these features. In form, it represents the old vernacular building arrangement which was commonplace in the Scottish landscape before the improvements of the 18th and 19th centuries. It was a tradition continued, however, in the new townships formed during the phase of crofting establishment.

To facilitate the winnowing process, in which the chaff was blown away from the threshed grain, barns sometimes had doors deliberately facing one another, so that a good draught could whistle through between them as the crofter tossed the grain and husks up into the air. At its simplest, threshing was accomplished with a simple flail, consisting of a bit of wood attached to a longer wooden handle by a short piece of rope or leather. When brought smartly down upon a sheaf of grain, it released the seed heads from the straw and the chaff from the grain itself. Flails survived in use until comparatively recent times. In the 1960s I often encountered examples in northern barns. Grain drying was accomplished in a stone-built kiln in which a peat fire was lit. This might be a free-standing affair, or, as in the case of the Northern Isles, a beautifully rounded appendage of the barn.

Small hand querns continued to find a use at the end of the last century, providing yet another link with ancient times when stone querns were employed. But their output was little in relation to the amount of hand labour required to turn the wheel, so water mills were inevitably preferred. The small horizontal mills which ground down the oats for feeding the family could be found in crofting communities in both Northern and Western Isles. Earlier antiquarians referred to them as Norse mills. Their presence was directly related to the availability of water power on a flowing burn to turn the horizontal wheel. Such was the scarcity of suitable sites and the need for a means of milling the grain that some burns might have a series of mills built along them. A few survived until comparatively recent times in Shetland and Lewis, but the best known is the one at Dounby in Orkney. Known there as a 'click' mill for the sound that emanated from it when milling was in progress, the Dounby mill is now a preserved monument. Like the Arnol blackhouse, it is a tangible reminder of the way things were at the basic level of crofting life last century. From the mill, the ground-down oatmeal was transferred to the house where it was stored in a dry wooden chest for use throughout the winter, spring and following summer. Disaster attended any failure of the grain harvest, and crofters were no strangers to crop failure in such an uncertain environment.

As the meal girnal demonstrates, the interior furnishing and plenishings of the old houses were minimal and decidedly functional. Some seating, the necessary bedding arrangements, a table and a dresser fulfilled the needs of the folk. Where flagstone or even schist was used as a building medium, various keeping places were provided in the stonework in perpetuation of a tradition which can be noted in the houses of the earliest island folk of countless centuries ago. When geese were an important part of the northern island economy, an alcove was even provided at ground level for the broody goose to hatch her eggs while day-to-day family life continued around her.

By the last century, imported heavy and well-patterned crockery from the south had become the crofter wife's pride and joy on the dresser. Earlier generations made do with more basic local things. In Caithness, flagstone plates were once used, and home-fired pottery produced the old handthrown highland *crogain* or pots used for storing milk. These functional vessels had a history of use from Iron Age times — yet another expression of the continuity of culture which gave 19th-century crofters such links with their most ancient forebears. The Lewis parish of Barvas was famed last century for the pottery pieces which were produced there, some of them in imitation of designs from southern potteries and highly collectable by visitors of the time, including members of the Napier Commission. Wood and horn were also employed for kitchen utensils, both being shaped into spoons.

At the heart of family living was the hearth with the peat fire which was never allowed to go out. It was a glowing symbol of the continuity of life in home and community, so that the quenching of the fires with water by those who came to carry out the work of eviction last century was all the more poignant.

Where there was no chimney, it was an advantage for the seating to be low, since the peat reek was reluctant to disperse, and hung in a blue haze below the roof. Beds were invariably of the box type which, if wooden, could be moved, but if wall-built were part of the very structure of the dwelling. Where flagstone was employed for wall construction, beds could easily be built into the depth of the walls, and sometimes they were even outshot, meaning that the stone-built bedding place actually projected out from the line of the house wall.

The family diet was of the most basic, with oatmeal as its staple. For crofters along the coastal fringe and in the islands, herring provided a high protein accompaniment and could be salted down in barrels of brine for winter use. An alternative form of preservation of fish was to dry them on blowy summer days. The darker bere meal was also used to make the bannocks which have remained a characteristic part of the diet of crofting's Nordic province. Before the hottering teapot took its place at every fireside, home-produced ale was the normal domestic drink, the quality of the home brew being a matter of much domestic pride.

It is easy to conjure up a couthie picture of 19th-century crofting life with the folk gathered for a ceilidh by the cheery glow of peat fire and the spluttering flame of a fish-oil cruisie lamp. At the other end, the romantic image is completed by the soft-eyed cows munching contentedly in their stalls while the thatch and deep walls deaden the howling of the wind outside. Indeed, some 19th-century travellers had their books illustrated with pictures which emphasised just such contented couthieness in interiors of Highland homes.

The reality behind this image of cosy cohabitation was that the beasts spent the winter on top of a steadily accumulating, urine-sodden heap of dung in the byre end, and that folk shared the sanitary arrangements with their livestock. In an age

Croft museum, Skye. The distinctive ways of the crofting past are part of the attraction for visitors to the North and West.

where tuberculosis and other serious diseases were endemic, the domestic living conditions did little for the health of crofter folk. Small wonder, then, that those improving leases being offered to tenants in Lewis at the end of the last century specifically required that dwelling houses have at least two apartments, and that the cattle byre be separate altogether. It was long past time for change.

Changes did come, of course. Kitchen and sleeping accommodation were separated off, and livestock banished to a separate byre. Yet the old ways were slow in dying, and it was a constant source of wonder to visitors to the islands that the blackhouse tradition was maintained for so long. Throughout the crofting counties, townships continued as a strong repository for the skilled traditions of vernacular building. Even today, crofters may still give their barns a fresh topping of straw and pin the thatch down with chicken wire or an old fish net in a last imitation of the practised skills of their forefathers. Only a few decades ago, hundreds of croft houses retained their traditional roof covering, and it was often the incongruity of the scene that took the eye, as when an old-style television aerial stuck prominently out of the thatch.

Recently, I was presented with a striking contrast as I was ushered into an inhabited thatched house of the old type. The double walls were almost seven feet thick in all, so that in the low angle of the evening sun, the small windows were like tunnels, admitting little direct light. It was the winking green digits of the video recorder in the darkness that took my eye. Sir Arthur Mitchell's book was called *The Past in the Present*. Here, so strikingly presented, was the advanced technology of the present in the setting of a vernacular building rooted in an ancient past.

CHAPTER 10

Crofting ways

Joke: 'Did you hear about the crofter who gave himself a hernia lifting the heavy creel off his wife's back?'

Such quips about the role of women in crofting society are not uncommon. Unfortunately, they betray a lack of understanding of the way in which the crofters' way of life has functioned. Present crofting ways have evolved out of a pattern that was little different from the subsistence economies of today's third world where the *raison d'être* of living is the securing of the family food supply, in a very direct and practical way. Failure to achieve the necessary level of productivity is followed by inevitable want and starvation.

In coastal communities, where the menfolk were likely to be away at sea for long periods, there was little option but for the women to attend to the chores of running the croft as well as having the responsibility of raising a family. Thus their share in the work was, of necessity, a considerable one. Carrying a laden creel of heavy, wet seaweed up from the shore was no more unusual a part of women's work than knitting socks or baking bannocks.

In such a close relationship with the land, the work of the croft was in fundamental harmony with the seasons of the year, and was performed by a range of tried and tested equipment. Apart from farming tasks, the casting of peats for winter fires was a widespread annual activity. Places which were unfortunate enough to lack this resource had to find substitute fuel supplies, dried cow dung and tangles being used to supplement peat supplies boated in from other locations.

Peat continues to be cut for fuel using the specialised cutter with an angled blade to form blocks which are then dried in the wind before carting off to form the winter peat stack. A well-formed peat stack is in itself an expression of a traditional skill. In some places machines are now in use which extrude wet peat in small cylindrical lumps. This is less demanding in labour, but the result is much poorer than the traditional spade-cut product.

Using Shetland ponies to cart home the winter fuel supply on the island of Unst.

As a cultivating instrument on the farming land, the *caschrom* (literally 'crooked foot') once found a widespread use throughout West Coast crofting communities. It consisted of a heavy metal blade fixed on to the end of a long wooden handle. A projecting piece of the blade allowed strong foot purchase to turn heavy soils made sodden by the rain — a commodity with which most of the crofting province is bountifully blessed.

The *caschrom* became an essential tool in working the uneven and rocky ground of the west where the cultivable land lay in scattered irregular patches, often with little depth of soil to mask the ancient bedrock below. The *cas dhireach* was the delving spade, used in the construction of the lazy beds or *feannagan* whose abandoned outlines mark so many island and coastal landscapes today, though their active use has passed away. Lazy beds are long ridges formed by removing the ground from one side of a line to create a double thickness in areas where deep soils were scarce. This, coupled with generous inputs of seaweed from the shore, was the basis of food crop

Horizontal or 'Norse' corn grinding mills on a Shetland burn. In the Outer Hebrides there existed a vast terminology of Gaelic words associated with these small mills.

production. At the same time, the arrangement helped give much needed drainage. The lazy bed technique is a feature of other parts of the Celtic fringe, for I have seen the same response on the Irish Aran Islands off the Galway coast where the problem is an almost total lack of soil over the bare grey expanses of limestone pavement.

The *caschrom* continued to find some application here and there up until surprisingly recent times. Its long survival may be seen not so much as a quaint anachronism in out of the way situations, but as the continuation of a long tradition, and the retention of a tool appropriate to the job in particular circumstances. The contemporary phrase 'appropriate techno-logy' clearly had an application in the crofting situation decades ago. Some evocative pictures of use of the *caschrom* survive in photographic archives. Museums with crofting relics preserve some examples, and visitors to the Captain's Cabin in Ullapool can see a *caschrom* accompanied by photographs demonstrating its use.

The *caschrom*, as the Gaelic name would imply, was essentially a tool of the Gaidhealtachd. But there were northern parallels in the manner of cultivating the ground. On Shetland crofts, the delling spade was widely employed in working the small cultivation rigs which patterned the edges of the voes. The Shetland spade was a wooden handle about four feet long with a stout metal blade and a foot peg sticking out above it, enabling the user to get a firm purchase on the implement when turning the crop ground. Its use was frequently organised into 'delling teams' in that spirit of cooperative endeavour so characteristic of crofting townships everywhere.

Sometimes the delling spade was used to raise up ridges for growing potatoes, but it was on the west coast and in the Western Isles that lazy beds really left their mark on the landscape, and their impress is to be seen there yet. Long abandoned, their outlines still draw the eye and kindle the imagination, for they are mute memorials to the life and times of the folk who laboriously raised them up and coaxed a living out of them. They have largely ceased to have a role in the crofting scene, but even in their state of abandonment, they remain a powerful presence on Hebridean hill slopes now returned to grass and rush, the more accentuated of them suggesting the long green graves of recumbent giant forms.

Lazy beds were, to an extent, a response to a high rainfall environment, as well as a solution to the problem of restricted soil depth. In the northern crofting landscape, the response to local climate also found expression in the form of the drystane *planticrues* built out on open northern moors. In these the vulnerable young cabbage plants were reared. *Planticrues* were square stone-built enclosures a few feet wide and long. Completely gateless, their role was to offer much needed shelter from blasting island winds, at the same time affording protection from hungry sheep and cattle.

The flagstone building and roofing tradition is richly expressed in this Orkney barn and corn drying kiln.

I once watched a Shetland crofter prepare a planticrue by placing thick fresh sods, soil side up, into the base of the small stone enclosure. He explained how his crofting forebears used to put a handful of seed into their mouths, take a generous gulp of water from a jug, then proceed to spit out the whole lot in a controlled but forceful manner. In past times, when the menfolk were often bearded, the filtering effect of a well-whiskered face was apparently something of an inconvenience when performing this task! *Planticrues* for the same sort of purpose were also a feature of the low-lying north isles of Orkney and occasionally elsewhere. In latter days, planticrues have found some use as sheltered vegetable plots, with additional barricades placed above their drystane walls to discourage the more determined sheep.

Today's crofter homes are well served by deep freezes for preserving out of season food, but in the past other methods had to be sought to ensure the availability of summer's bounty in the unproductive days of winter. Splitting and drying fish in the open air is a long-established practice, as is curing by smoke. I recall once having tea in the homely setting of a crofter's kitchen in Dunrossness where the pulley suspended from the ceiling sported several pairs of hand-knitted socks at one end and some matching pairs of home-smoked haddocks at the other.

But some island crofter folk turned to their stone-studded land for an answer to the food preservation problem. This was how the celebrated *cleitan* on St Kildan came into being. Behind the village street of Hirta lies a great scatter of turf-topped little stone cells used for the preservation of dried seabird carcases and other foodstuffs. The sea breezes might filter freely through the drystane walls, but the damaging damp and salt spray were firmly excluded. Among the Northern Isles, the island of Swona once had a similar tradition.

Utilising nature's bounty in the seasonal harvest of birds' eggs and young seabirds has been a long-established tradition, especially on remoter island communities where the opportunities were greater and the constraints on producing food from the land more tight. Even today, in a last echo of that seasonal wildlife harvesting that once supplemented the diet of island folk, the men of Ness in Lewis go on their annual gathering trip to remote Sula Sgeir to bring back the carcases of *gugas* or young gannets, though they are hardly driven to do so now by the pressing need that once sent men scrambling over the dizzy heights of towering island cliffs. Such is the appeal of this acquired taste from the past that demand may exceed supply when the boat returns with the birds, though the attraction of a well-seasoned guga is one that only an islander can truly appreciate.

Smallness of scale in island places called for its own human response, and cooperative effort was always the community keyword at periods of greatest need, as when harvest time came round. One of my enduring personal recollections of communal crofting work is of squads of Shetland crofters out in small corn rigs under glorious island skies, each one busy at the scything or binding or stooking, the whole group itself tightly bound by the ties of community life which characterised crofting society and was so much heightened by small island living.

At the heart of the communality of crofting is the shared

Grinding quern and flail for thrashing oats outside a Northern Isles barn.

grazing. The common grazings and scattalds are part of the crofters' inheritance from the past. They persist in an age when shared ways of land holding and working have been consigned to the realms of social history in more southerly places, where commons were also once widespread. The individual share or souming is a regulated allotment of grazing, so that the croft's livestock-producing potential is not constrained solely by the small scale of its inbye croft land.

It falls to elected township grazing committees to oversee and regulate the common grazings in the community interest. The importance of the common grazings to the crofting townships was made clear in the records of the evidence presented to the Napier Commission. In well-peopled districts with small individual allocations of farming land, the right to pasture livestock on the common grazings was of paramount importance, and its removal nothing short of a disaster. In addition, the commons provided fuel and a source of building materials, so that their importance to the life of the crofting community should not be underestimated.

Sometimes the grazings might be at some distance from the townships. In these cases there came into play a practice shared by folk in upland areas throughout Europe. The Irish and Welsh had their summer grazings throughout their upland districts. In Switzerland, folk made their way up to the high summer alps, and in Norway cattle were driven to the high saeter grazings. In a Norwegian valley in the late 1960s, to the background tinkling of cow bells, I watched an elderly woman herding her horned brown and white Telemark milking cattle over the slopes above the tree-line. She was one of the last upholders in her district of a disappearing valley tradition. In the Long Island the practice of taking the milking cows to the shieling survived longest of all, and memories are alive yet of the anticipation of the exodus to the *airigh*, a welcome escape from the routine of township life in the long summer days.

This transhumance, as this yearly movement of man and beast is called, is the seasonal transfer of livestock — usually cattle — to summer grazings well removed from the cultivated lands. In this way the all-important winter hay crop could be secured, free from the depredations of wandering stock.

In Lewis, until surprisingly recent times, the shelters of the folk were turf and stone affairs that served only the short-term needs of accommodation. To visit the area west of Stornoway today is to come upon a scatter of bothies and shacks in varying states of repair. Some are used as summer retreats; others provide shelter and a place to brew the tea when out at the peats.

As well as removing the livestock from the farming areas, transhumance grew out of the need to supplement the output of the township lands. The scarcity of such grazings in well-peopled places led to the practice of pasturing stock on outlying islands and holms, sometimes in quite difficult circumstances. Fair Islanders made use of the grazings on top of the towering offshore mass of Sheep Craig. A chain fixed into the rock was used to reach the top for the *rooing* or plucking of wool and removal of surplus stock, an annual event that continued into the 1970s. Apart from the continued keeping of native sheep in

Crofter preparing a planticrue in Shetland. Such stone-walled enclosures provided a sheltered environment for the growing of cabbages.

the shore in Orkney's northernmost isle, sheep are also grazed on small holms where seaweed is an essential element of their diet. One of the most interesting adaptations to the use of such places, with their attendant dangers of sheep being washed away by the incoming tide, is on one small holm where a stone-built 'fort' allows sheep to take refuge when the tide is high and their seaweed grazings immersed. Elsewhere, sheep continue to be flitted back and fore between small islands, but the constraints of time, cost and a regard for human safety is drawing this long-established practice to a close in many places.

Although croft work was always demanding of human effort, animal power could take some of the strain and lighten the load. Horses were employed to carry out the work of land preparation. In the west, garrons provided power for ploughing, harrowing and bringing in the harvests of inbye land, shore and hill in the form of hay and corn, seaweed and peats. Now largely redundant in their original role, interest centres more on these native highland ponies for leisure pursuits. Recently, in this age of enthusiasm for rare breeds, some effort has been put into preserving the distinctive Eriskay pony type after its numbers had fallen to a dangerously low level. Until comparatively recent times, the Department of Agriculture maintained a fine stud of Highland ponies on its farm outside Inverness, loaning good quality stallions to crofters for serving working mares, thus maintaining a good type.

Orkney crofters last century worked with ponies derived from imports of Highland garrons shipped across from Caithness. Oxen were yoked to the plough and the practice lasted right up to the 1950s in the Northern Isles, but on the better lands the bigger scale of working allowed the use of Clydesdales for tilling the ground. The sturdy Shetland pony was capable of surprising strength when put to the plough or harnessed to harrow, and, like the garron, brought home the winter fuel supply from distant peat banks. Now, however, the island pony sales allow crofters to sell 'Shelties' not for croft work or for labouring in the dark depths of coal mines as they used to do, but for children's riding animals or simply for hobby livestock.

As times moved on and more mechanised ways were introduced, the crofters' dependable ponies became displaced by the reliable Ferguson tractors. The little grey 'Fergie' was ideally suited to its role in carting and small-scale cultivation around the croft, and even today, decades after its introduction into the crofting scene, the familiar grey form in varying states of decrepitude can be seen around countless houses and byres wherever crofting takes place.

As a complement to the tractor in more recent times, the binder has continued to find a use in harvesting the oat crop, throwing out the bound grain sheaves to be stooked and left in the hope of wind drying them for the ingathering. Mainland dealers found a steady island trade in the binders which advancing technology had rendered obsolescent in more intensively-worked places, but which still had a part to play in the less sophisticated ways of crofting agriculture.

The vagaries of climate have always severely limited the crofter's choice of how the land might be used. In a poor summer, haymaking can be a real trial in such a moist and cloudy climatic regime, and prolonged wet conditions can reduce the precious winter feed crop to a blackened mass scarcely

In Lewis the shieling system survived long after its demise elsewhere. To the west of Stornoway is a scatter of bothies, many still used by peat cutters.

worth the ingathering. In recent years, island crofters have been reduced to importing hay from distant places to augment their megre home-produced fodder resources — an expensive business in an age of ever increasing sea freight charges.

From an ecological point of view, traditional practices of working the croft land involving small-scale haymaking have been extremely beneficial. For example, partly as a result of the survival of traditional ways of managing croft land, the western crofting fringe has become the last refuge of the corncrake, and from a botanical viewpoint, the machair lands continue to support an interesting and colourful range of wild flowers now banished from reclaimed lands.

But it is not just in tradition and in a fascinating legacy of material remains that the crofting areas provide an interest. There is a living dimension, too, for crofters made their own contribution to the country's rich heritage of native livestock breeds. The Shetland cow is a small, black and white dual-purpose breed well suited to the northern crofting environment

Bull of the old Shetland breed. The tethering of livestock has been a feature of crofting areas where grazing is in unfenced rigs and patches.

in which it evolved. Great efforts have recently been made to assure its future, after the near complete demise of the breed in its native island home, although there is some renewed local interest and stock has recently been selected for the windswept Falkland Islands.

Shetland sheep remain an important part of the northern crofting economy, being renowned for the fine quality of fleeces produced from rough island grazings. Unusual colour patterns were once prevalent throughout the scattalds, ranging from the rich brown of the *moorit* to the unusual *katmogit* where the belly colour was different from the rest of the body. Falling prices for coloured fleeces have encouraged crofters to breed out the more interesting colour variants in favour of the 'natural' shade.

North Ronaldsay, northernmost island of Orkney, still retains its large flock of native sheep living their strangely maritime existence outside the massive sheep dyke. These salty-fleeced

Scything and binding the harvest on Fair Isle. Such bonds of cooperation at times of need have been a hallmark of the crofting community.

beasts live in groups which recognise their own stretch of shore — their *clowgang* — beyond which they are reluctant to stray, making the driving of them along the beach an experience frustrating to experience but amusing to observe. At appointed times, sheep *punds* are announced by some suitable signal and there then ensues a communal round-up of the sheep for clipping. Individual ownership of these old island sheep is recognised by an interesting range of lug marks, a practice used among crofters everywhere. Horn brands have also been a useful means of individual marking, as the door of the blacksmith's shop in Stornoway used to show, for it was covered with all the different brand marks.

Lewis blackface sheep are distinctly different from their mainland cousins, and on the rock-girt outlier of Boreray there is a curious remnant of the old black-faced stock left behind after the islanders departed from St Kilda in 1930. The ancient brown Soay sheep from the same island group are perhaps now more familiar from farm parks and animal collections up and down the land than from the seabird-enriched grazings of their homeland.

Naturally, today's crofters are influenced by the same economic trends that prevail in farming elsewhere, and so the long-established Cheviot and black-face stock gives way to Suffolks or whatever breeds are considered capable of making a contribution to incomes. The spotty-fleeced Jacob's sheep has even found a use on some crofts as provider of distinctively patterned skins for curing and selling.

Crofting townships have in the past used native bulls such as Aberdeen Angus and Shorthorn, often on loan from the Department of Agriculture, but the township bull is as likely to be a continental Simmental these days as a native breed. The loaned-out beasts from the Department were transferred to pastures new when their paternity was judged to be sufficiently impressed on the local stock.

Transporting bulls to island places is a task fraught with difficulties as obstreperous and very bulky individuals are persuaded into making undignified boat passages. In recent times, the national media had a field day in reporting the sorrowful tale of the posthumous bovine hero of the Hebrides, who hit the national headlines when he foundered while being towed over the sea on his way to a new posting.

With rising prices of stock feed, crofters are just as likely to buy in their egg supplies these days as to keep their own poultry, but if they do it is most likely to be the brown hybrid egg producers which now dominate the national flock. Indeed, one crofter in Skye yearly supplies young replacement laying stock throughout the north. With the need for home raising of chicks thus removed, the croft flock is often bereft of male company. So the traveller whose knowledge of crofting has been influenced by reading a certain type of popular literature, and who comes expecting to find the cockerel firmly constrained by a covering basket lest its improprieties in the hen harem should offend on the Sabbath day, is likely to be doomed to disappointment.

In past times, however, eggs were an important item of barter for crofter wives, and Orkney crofts added their own con-tribution to the huge farm output of the islands. The fearsome hurricane of January 1952 was the beginning of the end for island egg-producing, however, when so many places lost hens and henhouses into the sea. Such was the severity of the blast that on some of the islands they shovelled the corpses up by the barrowful along the shore. During the last century, crofters' geese were herded on the common grazings of the Northern Isles in great numbers, though their days have also gone. In fact, on some Shetland scattalds the grazing of geese is strictly forbidden in the existing regulations.

At the present time, things are far from static in the livestock scene, for, among today's crofters, the potential of such things as red deer venison or even angora goat fleeces is ensuring a continuing new dimension to crofting agriculture.

CHAPTER 11

The organisation of crofting

Of the true nature of crofting, misconceptions abound. What it is not is some relic form of peasant agriculture doggedly surviving along the remote Atlantic ends of Europe. Neither is it some system of 'good life' subsistence farming where families somehow manage to live off what their croft land can produce. Nor is a croft just the dwelling house of the crofting family, though that is one of the common perceptions of the term.

Crofting today is a way of life that is distinctive in its character. In places, it is true that ageing of the population has been accompanied by declining vigour in the working of the land. But circumstances vary widely, and where crofting is at its most robust, as it is among crofters in the younger age groups, it is a way of life that is demanding in its commitment if it is to supply a family living.

Not every small landholding in the Highlands and Islands is strictly speaking a croft, though the word is often used in a fairly loose fashion to describe any kind of northern smallholding. To define a croft is at the same time simple and complex. In fact, crofting law is so beset by complexity that the subject is a metaphorical minefield for the unwary. In the precise and legal sense of the term a croft may be regarded as a unit of land that is registered by the Crofters Commission. In terms of its characteristics, however, although every croft has land-working as its basis, the way in which its occupants are supported are many and decidedly various.

There are approximately 17,700 crofts in townships located in the seven former counties of Argyll, Inverness, Ross & Cromarty, Sutherland, Caithness, Orkney and Shetland. These are still known as the crofting counties. In statistical terms the pattern is strongly island-based, for the great majority of crofts are located outwith the mainland.

A strong feature of crofting is that the vast majority of crofts are held on a tenancy agreement with a landlord. The rent which crofter pays to landlord is for what is known as the 'bareland' only and is based on its worth before reclamation from what was frequently very difficult land. It is the crofter's own responsibility to provide a dwelling house and whatever other buildings are required. As tenants have exercised their legal right to seek to acquire ownership of the croft, the number of owner-occupiers has risen. Although in these circumstances he or she then technically ceases to be a crofter, the croft land continues to be subject to the provisions of the Crofting Acts.

There is a wag's definition of a croft that is often quoted when the subject is being discussed. It defines a croft as 'a piece of land in the Highlands entirely surrounded by regulations'. Amusing though that might be, it is not hard to see how the whole business and social organisation that is crofting came to be so affected by regulation and legislation. Crofting must be considered against that unique pattern and legacy of social history which we have noted in previous chapters. Indeed, Scottish legal history was made quite recently with the publication of a substantial volume entirely devoted to crofting law, an indication of the scope and legal complexity of the subject.

At the heart of crofting affairs is the Crofters Commission with their headquarters in Inverness, the nearest large urban centre to most of the crofting province. The Commission was established in 1955, following on from the report of a Commission of Enquiry into Crofting Conditions, their remit being the administration of the Crofters (Scotland) Act 1955. This Act of Parliament was then amended by The Crofters (Scotland) Act 1961, and followed in the next decade by the Crofting Reform (Scotland) Act 1976. By this time, crofting had been set into such a comprehensive statutory framework that perhaps the wag's definition is not so far removed from the truth after all.

The main work of the present Crofters Commission is to 'reorganise, develop and regulate crofting in the crofting areas of Scotland, viz. the former counties of Shetland, Orkney, Caithness, Sutherland, Ross and Cromarty, Inverness and Argyll; to promote the interests of crofters there; and to keep under review all matters relating to crofting. In carrying out their functions the Commission are required to have regard to local circumstances and conditions.'

To demonstrate the commitment to the latter, the full-time chairman and six part-time members each has responsibility for a designated area of the Highlands and Islands. The Commission also appoint a panel of persons who are resident within the crofting province and who are able to assist the Commission by means of their local and practical knowledge of the areas they represent. In such a scattered and diverse part of the country, geographical conditions and local attitudes may vary considerably, so familiarity with the circumstances of different places and communities is important.

Though there are small scattered pockets of crofting in more separated mainland locations such as Speyside, Loch Ness-side, Easter Ross and the Black Isle, the greatest concentration by far is in the Western Isles (about 6,000), in Skye and other islands of the Inner Hebrides (1,800), in the north and west periphery of the Scottish mainland (2,300) and in Shetland (2,700).

Many areas of the eastern Highlands and in Orkney consist of productive farmland whose character is in marked contrast to the crofting scene of the west, while the interior lands of the Highlands are in vast expanses of upland sheep walks, deer forests, grouse moors or an increasing cover of forestry plantations. As a result, crofting actually occupies approximately one-fifth of the total land area of the Highlands and Islands and has a decidedly peripheral pattern around the country's outermost edge.

Despite its scattered distribution pattern, crofting no longer exists in isolation, whether it be in a geographical, economic or political sense, for the roads, air and sea routes which serve it are linked to the national communications network; its economy is tied to other parts of the country, and most of the area of the Highlands and Islands comes under the classification of a 'Less Favoured Area' under a directive of the European Economic Community. Indeed, in recent times the crofters have had cause to listen with interest to the decrees emanating from the political corridors of Strasbourg or Brussels, for many parts of the crofting province have reaped the benefit of United Kingdom membership of the European Community. In this way, old links and similarities with the Gaeltacht of Ireland have been renewed, for both areas are perceived to be

Improved inbye land with common grazing on the hill land above is a feature of the landscape throughout the crofting province.

peripheral regions where economic development is a particular challenge.

With the absorption of much of the most productive land into more economic farm units, crofting was left to survive as best it could in some of Scotland's poorest areas. For those who might be more familiar with the productive 'prairie' farmscapes of the more southerly parts of the realm, the idea of a landholding of one acre of improved ground might seem quite derisory, but such crofts do exist, though the average size is more in the region of around ten acres. In other parts of the developed world, of course, such as Japan, many country people do make a living by intensive cultivation of similarly sized or even smaller holdings, but the limiting environmental circumstances of land, soil and climate of the Scottish crofting province must be borne in mind.

In many crofting areas even the best quality arable land has low potential for crop growing, so the saving grace is the crofters' share in the rough grazing — usually hill land — held in common by all individuals in the townships. In addition, there are some places where groups of townships share further rights of grazing in other commons, as in the Ness area of Lewis where a considerable number of townships share a common grazing.

Perhaps above all, it is in this common grazing and the ways of its organisation that one can see the strongest link with that spirit of cooperative working and sharing which was once so much a part of the crofting scene. As time and technology together have changed the ways of working the land from a series of manual arts to a more solitary system of mechanical processes, the ways of communal working have tended to fade. The survival of the common grazing, therefore, is perhaps the most tangible link with days gone by. Associated with the grazings are the sheep stock clubs which operate in many areas. Crofters with shares in the club may employ a shepherd to manage their sheep as one communal flock, thereby creating some valuable local employment.

Taking the crofting area as a whole, there are no fewer than 800 common grazings and scattalds, although some of these are very small in extent with only a few crofters holding rights of pasturing livestock upon them. These fragmented commons are a particular feature of the Shetland crofting landscape where the large district scattald is complemented by small parcels of unimproved ground mixed in with the improved inbye land. In fact, there were no regulations for stocking the scattalds till after the Crofters Act of 1886.

The difficulties to which the lack of regulation of shares or soumings gave rise point to the problems which would exist if every crofter was intent on putting as many animals as he or she wanted on to a common grazing. The practice, therefore, is to regulate the stocking to the best advantage of all users. Nevertheless, despite regulation of common grazings, overgrazing can still be a problem in areas where deer and even wild goats compete with crofters' livestock. Indeed, the depredations of deer on crofting inbye land can create real difficulties, at a time when deer numbers throughout the Highlands currently stand at a very high level. As a consequence, the Crofters Commission works closely with the Red Deer Commission in dealing with problem situations as they arise.

Elections are held every three years to appoint grazings

committees whose task it is to oversee the use of the common lands. Indeed, so important is proper management of township grazings considered to be that the Crofters Commission arranged a first training course for grazings committee clerks at Portree in Skye in 1989.

The work of the grazings committee clerks involves such matters as setting the date on which sheep or other stock are moved from the crofts to the grazings, seeing to the provision and upkeep of fences and fanks, and the organisation of husbandry matters such as dipping and clipping. On an upland sheep farm such things are a matter of individual decision, but in a crofting community they must be decided by consensus.

The use of the law to enforce the statutory obligations of crofters is, in practice, so uncommon that a case heard at Dingwall Sheriff Court in January 1991 created considerable interest. The case involved two crofters who admitted failing to pay their share of the cost of building and replacing a township fank.

Generally speaking, the common grazings and scattalds are on hill land beyond the better lands that lie within the township dyke, but in the Western Isles, common grazings may be found down on the sandy machair where livestock can graze on the rich green seaside sward. The Orkney island of North Ronaldsay is a curious exception, on which the high sheep dyke separates off the interior farmlands from the common grazings of the shore, though in reality these are often merely rocky platforms of sea-washed flagstones where tangles flourish. Indeed, grazings anywhere which contain a stretch of shore can be quite valuable, for seaweed provides a useful supplement to the diet and mineral intake of grazing sheep. When a crude oil spillage polluted the waters round some Shetland shores a number of years ago, it was no surprise to read in press accounts that the wildlife casualties included seabirds, otters and crofters' sheep.

Relics of the practice of runrig holding of land which was so widely abolished throughout Scotland last century continue to persist here and there in a few west coast and Western Isles' parishes. In the latter, areas of flat sandy land on the machair were allocated in runrig strips, giving everyone in the township a chance of working some better land along with the inland ground of thin and peaty soils.

In the Northern Isles, examples of 'rig aboot' cultivation have survived until recent times, with two adjacent crofts sharing the land in an alternating allocation of rigs. Sometimes the reasons for the survival of such outdated practices have simply been the reluctance of ageing crofters to seek any change. In this sense, the situation might be said to resemble that in some parts of western Europe where fragmentation of the farmscape evolved out of that same desire for fairness in land allotment as well as from a legacy of subdivisions. In continental areas too, the drive towards consolidation of land into more viable units has been hindered by reluctance on the part of older members of the community to change the landholding practices of a lifetime.

Even now, in the 1990s, the Crofters Commission may be called upon from time to time to consider requests for apportionment of runrig land. Nowadays, such last remnants are usually but a faint echo of the way things used to be when whole communities ballotted for their strips of land in a manner that can have been little removed from that of biblical times when the Psalmist remarked that the lines had fallen for him in pleasant places. Perhaps his favourable land allocation was in the Holy-Land equivalent of the machair.

Each year the Commission receives many requests for apportionment of common grazings where crofters wish to add a specific part of land to their croft. As always, a decision on whether to grant apportionment will only be made after consideration of the community interest. The Commission also deals with the matter of 'decrofting' of land when some local community interest is involved as, for example, in road widening or the provision of a playing field.

It is not in the nature of crofting to provide full-time employment or to generate sufficient income to support a family. The number of crofters making a full-time living off their croft is very small indeed; at the present time the figure stands at approximately 5%. As the Crofters Commission has recently stated: 'Crofting must be regarded as the anchor of population in an area of great scenic beauty and high environmental quality but with poor employment opportunities.' Crofters must therefore boost their incomes from a number of subsidiary occupations.

Statistics, as everyone knows, can be misleading, and no

Crofting township, Skye. The Crofters Commission oversees matters relating to crofting in this and hundreds of other townships throughout its designated area.

more so than in crofting where the number of registered crofts tends to suggest a situation which does not exist. In fact, although there are 17,700 crofts, that total is greatly in excess of the actual number of crofters. This anomaly has arisen because so many crofters have multiple tenancies, that is to say one person has more than one croft.

As the present-day representatives of a line of folk for whom conditions were once harsh and unfair in the extreme, today's crofters are protected by a code of inalienable and distinctive rights and conditions that is their inheritance from the struggles of those who lived in those difficult days and gave their eloquent testimonies to the Napier Commission.

Clearly, as a form of land use, crofting has an agricultural base. For the most part this consists of the production of young sheep and cattle (stores) for the more favoured lowland areas where farmers can fatten and finish them off for the market on their better grazings. As such, the crofting province continues to play its part in the overall pattern of food production in Scotland.

There are many problems involved in the rearing and finishing of livestock in Scotland's peripheral areas. The cost of bringing in fodder and of sending out stock together reduce the profit margins for the crofter. At the extreme is the situation faced, say, by a crofter in one of Shetland's isolated islands. Sheep being marketed from the island must first make the journey to Shetland Mainland by small boat and then be transported by road to Lerwick before being loaded on to the ship for Aberdeen. With steadily rising fodder and fuel costs, livestock rearing in remote areas must come ever closer to the edge of profitability, a situation that is a characteristic of crofting, and makes the need for subsidiary income the more essential.

To offset the disadvantages, however, the crofter has the benefit of some assistance schemes. EEC support for sheep and cattle production is administered for the benefit of crofters through the Scottish Office Agriculture and Fisheries Department (formerly the Department of Agriculture and Fisheries for Scotland). In an age when those who work the land are being encouraged to seek ways of diversifying their enterprises, grant schemes are available to encourage crofters to expand into non-agricultural activities, provided that they continue to work their croft land.

The Crofting Counties Agricultural Grants Scheme is administered by the Crofters Commission. This encourages agricultural advance by individual crofters or grazings committees through schemes of reseeding of grazing land, shelter belt provision, and a variety of other land improvement activities.

The Department of Agriculture and Fisheries for Scotland also have a number of schemes aimed at improving the overall quality of livestock within the crofting province. To this end, they operate their loan service for quality bulls and rams as well as an artificial insemination scheme in the Western Isles.

Should some project designed to improve agricultural productivity, such as the purchase of new tractors or machinery, not qualify under the foregoing schemes, the Highlands and Islands Development Board could institute assistance through its own grant or loan scheme. Indeed, the improvement in livestock marketing can be seen as one of the real success stories for crofting agriculture in recent times.

Latterly, the development strategy has been to target designated areas of the crofting counties for improvement schemes. Programmes of short-term development aimed at specific parts may be funded by EEC cash as part of their policy towards peripheral areas. The Integrated Development Programme for the Western Isles and the Agricultural Development Programme for the Scottish Islands (except the Western Isles) have been significant examples.

Two schemes targeted at smaller geographical areas have also been initiated. These programmes were set up by the Highlands and Islands Development Board in order to stimulate an island and a comparatively remote mainland situation respectively. The Skye Development Programme was formulated as a scheme to assist small-scale crofting agriculture and to encourage cooperative ventures, with special emphasis on inbye land improvement, better livestock management and increased local production of winter keep. The latter venture is significant in an area which has come to rely heavily on supplies of winter fodder being brought in at considerable cost. In an island situation, the obvious consequence of this is a further erosion of profit margins that may push the croft even closer to the edge of viability. In the past, development in crofting communities has been rather piecemeal, so recent aims have been to encourage well-planned and comprehensive developments that are likely to improve the productivity of crofts.

It is significant that, at this time, the HIDB (now assimilated into Highlands and Islands Enterprise) has been seeking to promote that feature of crofting which for so long gave it its distinctive character; its cooperative working of the land. As agricultural and general community activities have become less labour-intensive, the old tradition of communal working has greatly diminished. Now special inducements exist in the Skye DP for developments undertaken by two or more crofters. As in other European areas like Denmark, a key to the continuing viability of smaller-scale land units has been the fostering of a cooperative spirit, so that economies of scale can be enjoyed within a cooperative system. Small-scale individuality is thus

Old and new building types are often juxtaposed, as in this Lewis crofting township.

maintained within an economic system that favours the larger producer. And so, in this scheme, crofters with small areas of better inbye land have been encouraged to pool their resources of land, labour or capital.

The North West Development Programme was launched as a five-year HIDB initiative with a similar aim, that of helping crofters improve their long-term prospects and thus encouraging viability. The scheme covers one of the more remote parts of mainland Britain: the north-west parishes of Farr, Tongue, Durness, Edrachilles and Assynt in Sutherland, along with the part of Lochbroom parish to the north of the Ullapool River. An interesting feature of the NWDP and a sign of the environmentally-conscious age in which we live is that, along with obvious organisations like the Scottish Crofters' Union and the Department of Agriculture for Scotland, the Nature Conservancy Council and the Countryside Commission for Scotland were also consulted. This scheme offers financial incentives for both the agricultural and non-agricultural

enterprises which crofters might have. Recognising the importance of encouragement to the younger sector of the community
who are more likely to be innovative and go-ahead in their
thinking, special financial incentives are given to younger
crofters.

In February 1991, a new Rural Development Programme was
launched, its purpose being to breathe new hope and life into
economically fragile areas of the Highlands and Islands. Unlike
the previous development programmes of the 1980s which
concentrated on promoting traditional land use, the new
initiative is aimed specifically at crofters and other land occupiers
who are prepared to diversify their interests. These might
include such things as deer or shellfish farming, market
gardening or mushroom culture, but any suitable possibility is
considered. Marketing, for so long a major constraint in the
Highlands and Islands, is given a high profile in the scheme,
and particular encouragement is offered to those who are
prepared to work together.

The quality of crofter housing was for long a cause for concern.
The contrast between the old traditional style of house and its
modern, plain bungalow-type replacement has already been
commented upon. Crofters may qualify for grant and loan
assistance when building or improving a house, and this may
also include the provision of additional accommodation for
tourists. The replacements offer a comfortable home with
facilities equal to those found in more environmentally-favoured
areas. It is left to the surviving, superseded dwellings of past
crofter generations to express that close relationship with the
land and response to environment which the old vernacular
buildings so clearly demonstrated.

CHAPTER 12

The crofting province today

Geography imposes its own problems on crofting communities everywhere. It is in the nature of crofting life that isolation and insularity are common circumstances, and it should be recalled that the crofting population is predominantly an island-based one. In human terms, these circumstances find expression in long, complicated and costly journeys, in reduced provision of services, and in high freight charges for incoming goods or outgoing stock.

Communities on the Highland mainland may be equally disadvantaged in a land where detours dominate. While many tourists are drawn by island-hopping and by the attraction which remote areas have to offer, many more must be daunted by the time and cost involved in such journeyings.

In the Western Isles, Caledonian MacBrayne operate shipping services from Oban to the islands of Mull, Colonsay, Coll and Tiree. The fishing port of Mallaig provides the connection with the small isles. Services out of Oban go north-westwards to Castlebay in Barra and to Lochboisdale in South Uist. From Uig in Skye, CalMac operates services to Lochmaddy and to Tarbert in Harris. Ullapool has long since replaced the railhead at Kyle of Lochalsh as the mainland terminal for shipping services to Stornoway in Lewis.

The interested visitor standing at the pierhead at Oban or Ullapool cannot fail to be aware of the sheer nature of the dependence of island communities on mainland supplies. A few minutes spent observing the loading of a ferry will confirm that the days of self-sufficient island living are long gone. Even milk is shipped in bulk by tanker lorry to the islands in an age when the economics of maintaining a milk cow on the croft compare unfavourably with obtaining a regular supply from a creamery, even a mainland one, or from the local shop in the form of the long-life version. Centralisation of retail supply can also be seen at its most basic in the importation of supplies of mass-produced bread.

The construction of island piers has removed the need for laborious boating of essential supplies.

As carriers of passengers, livestock and freight, Caledonian MacBrayne have been cast in the all-important role of connecting link for many island communities, though those same communities do not necessarily see eye to eye with company decisions, as when CalMac announced the controversial proposals for Sunday sailings to Tarbert in Harris and met with threats of a fishing boat blockade.

At a more local level, many smaller islands depend on their own links with larger neighbours. Raasay has its boat connection with Skye, which in turn has a frequent link with Kyle of Lochalsh on the mainland. The island of Scalpay off Harris's eastern shore is populous enough to have a service with a car ferry of sufficient size to allow travelling shops to cross over from Tarbert.

Eriskay and Berneray are dependent on sea links still, but insularity has gradually declined throughout the Western Isles as a result of the provision of fixed links in the form of bridges or causeways. This has the effect of 'tying' island communities together, and of creating clusters of linked island groups which can be more effectively serviced. Benbecula was joined, out of strategic need, with its larger neighbour South Uist during the last war. To complete the geographical integration of the island cluster, Benbecula was then connected to North Uist by way of the small island of Grimsay in 1960. The advantages of such island integration have been clearly demonstrated in both economic and social terms, permitting goods to pass easily, allowing access to jobs, and fostering contact among once separated communities.

After the people of the island of Great Bernera on the west side of Lewis pressed their case for a fixed link, a bridge was built across Loch Roag in 1953 by Ross and Cromarty County Council. In recent times Comhairle nan Eilean, the Western Isles Island Council, has discussed the possibility of repeating its predecessor's effort with the offshore islands of Berneray, Eriskay and Scalpay.

In the meantime, Vatersay has recently achieved its desired connection with Barra, after suffering from the want of a car ferry. In a society so dependent on movement of people and goods by road, the lack of a vehicle ferry is undoubtedly a serious drawback. For a time, livestock were moved out of Vatersay by a barge, but when this went out of use the practice of swimming cattle across the Sound of Vatersay was resumed, until the incident of the drowning of the bull in 1987. Before completion of the causeway link, removing island livestock even to Barra was a costly and time-consuming exercise. In this latter part of the century, for Vatersay and the other remaining small islands devoid of fixed links, insularity has proved an expensive state of affairs to live with.

Indeed, Vatersay demonstrates all too clearly the difficulties faced by crofters in such small island situations. It is not hard to seek the reasons for the decline in the island population to 65 in 1988. Concerns over sea crossings for children attending secondary education, and over access to other social services, including medical provision, may weigh heavily on the minds of

Loading sheep on the Fair Isle mail boat in the 1960s. The marketing of livestock has always posed special problems for small island communities.

parents with children, and the loss of a single family from a small island community can be a serious problem for a primary school with an already precarious pupil roll. Ironically, the connection of Vatersay to Barra has threatened the continuing existence of the island's small primary school, with suggestions that the children travel the short distance to Castlebay instead, via the new causeway.

On a map of the crofting area, it is easy to pick out deserted islands where crofting communities once lived but where the realities of an isolated situation forced their own drastic solution to the problems of small island living. When populations decline to such a low level that the future of the school is called into question, it is the very heart of the island's future that is being threatened.

Once a population has dropped, even the quirks of nature may be serious, as on Fair Isle where, between 1930 and 1950, every baby (17 in all) born into the island was a boy. The resulting imbalance in population structure became a serious one, with a disproportionate number of islanders in the unmarried male category. This was not without its amusing side, however, for in the 1960s the island attracted a steady stream of journalists eager to do yet another story on Fair Isle's eligible bachelors. Among the ranks of the latter was one ageing crofter who performed a multitude of ancillary tasks to supplement his crofting income. These included some connection with officialdom as island receiver of wrecks should anything unexpected come ashore. When a tweedy female visitor from one of the southern ladies' magazines departed after doing the usual type of story, somebody suggested to the crofter that he had been a bit slow off the mark and had maybe missed his chance. 'Ah weel,' said he, after a bit of thought, 'Bit ye see, a'm no a receiver o' yon kind o' wreck!'

Distantly-located island communities such as Fair Isle and Foula in Shetland have had to take upon themselves a great deal of the responsibility for maintaining their boat links with Grutness and Walls respectively. But manning a mail boat effectively requires a population of able-bodied men from which to form a crew. Where fixed links are not an option, improvements to ferry connections may achieve considerable advantages. This has been the case in the north isles of Shetland where purpose-built roll-on roll-off ferries represent a tremendous advance on the previous situation with its small inter-island boats for passengers and light cargo, and the *Earl of Zetland* steamer which moved heavy goods and livestock.

Shetland is linked to Aberdeen by large passenger and cargo vessels of the P&O fleet which allow the export of crofter cattle and sheep to the north-east. The same company also operates the Pentland Firth crossing, where the *St Ola* maintains a regular connection between the Caithness port of Scrabster and Stromness. A small roll-on, roll-off ferry plies the Orkney South Isles route, while the North Isles are now served by two purpose-built ferries.

The farmers and crofters of Orkney's North Isles were served by steam navigation for a remarkable length of time. The old

Ferry leaving Harris for the island of Scalpay. Bridging the sea gap has been suggested, but insularity continues to impose its own problems for this and other crofting communities today.

coal-burning SS *Earl Sigurd* with her smoke-belching funnel was still serving the north isles in 1969 when her successor, the diesel-engined *Islander* took over.

Isolation should not necessarily be equated with insularity, however. Many mainland communities have had to suffer the same privations. Indeed, it might be argued that many such communities were less isolated at the end of the last century than they are now, for travel by water was then a way of life, and a plethora of small piers ensured that goods could be easily obtained by sea. Ordnance Survey maps of west coast sea lochs show the extent of this provision in the past. But now, in an age of road transport, piers and jetties lie redundant and in ruin, and the cost of improved road links — or even providing a road link for the first time — may be almost prohibitive. When the much-debated new road was opened up to the isolated crofter community of Rhenigidale in Harris, for example, the bill for constructing it came to over one million pounds.

Carrying the Saturday shopping from the mainland off the ferry at Kyleakin. The sea acts as a powerful physical and economic divide for island communities.

North-south communication along the seaboard of the western Highlands is difficult and disjointed, the direct result of the area's complicated geography. However, the Ballachulish Bridge in Argyll removed the need for the ferry crossing of the narrows or a time-consuming detour round Loch Leven, and the Kysesku Ferry crossing in Sutherland has also given way to a bridge at the entrance to Loch Glencoul, thus removing the frustrations suffered by local folk as they contemplated joining the tourist-swollen queues of vehicles waiting to board the ferry boat. The triple east-side bridging of the Dornoch, Cromarty and Beauly Firths has a significance for crofting communities in the far north, putting them in much closer touch by road with Inverness, the regional centre.

The most ambitious fixed link scheme by far, however, is for the bridge across to Skye. Though strong support has attended this project, local folk have been less than enchanted with the proposals for a toll crossing. At the same time, there has also

Post Office, Barvas. Such services are an important part of life in communities with a large proportion of elderly folk.

been a cooler reception from those who see the removal of Skye's insularity as representing a loss of identity and threat to its personality, since going 'over the sea to Skye' has long had a popular appeal to those from outside who do not have to make a living from crofting there.

Air travel has also assumed an important role for the remoter communities. Shetland, Orkney and the Inner and Outer Hebrides are all linked by air services into the domestic network. Even the lack of a proper airstrip has not prohibited the linking of Barra by air, for the sturdy Twin Otter plane operated by Loganair lands on its flat cockle strand at low tide, making flight schedules subject to tide conditions.

Even in pre-war days, the north isles of Orkney enjoyed a regular inter-island air service, and the name of Captain Fresson who flew the route in de Havilland Rapide biplanes has long been legendary in the islands. In those good old days, north isles' crofters could fly into Kirkwall for the day with baskets of produce to sell to the townsfolk. Fresson's present day successors are the Loganair pilots who fly their small Islander aircraft into a number of small island airstrips.

After some initial difficulties, such as the small planes skidding on the abundant cow pats left behind by livestock attracted to the grass strips in fields used as landing places, the inter-island air link got well and truly off the ground and has been serving island communities for more than two decades. In addition to providing a conventional passenger service which has been of the greatest benefit to north isles' folk, the aircraft are also able to carry urgently needed parts and spares for farming machinery. Island schools have also benefited from the availability of specialist teachers, and even a banking service has been operated by plane. In the isolated world of individual islands, the provision of air ambulance services have been of reassurance to hundreds of patients, not least the many expectant mothers who have had to make an unscheduled and speedy exit from their island homes.

Even the most remote of the Northern Isles enjoy the advantage of air contact. The sight and sound of a Loganair Islander aircraft droning its way into an island airstrip will instantly dispel any lingering imagining that island communities exist in a world of enforced isolation. In one case, even a world record is held. The island of Papa Westray has gone down in the record books as having the shortest scheduled air crossing. The total journey time from take-off to landing on its near neighbour, Westray, is a mere ten minutes!

One of the most marked and saddest features of crofting life over the past few decades has been the decline and ageing of the population. In landscape terms the result is the familiar reduction in active croft working, with rushes sprouting out of land that is all too obviously reverting to nature. For many aged township residents, crofting has become the mere maintenance of a sheep flock.

Lack of job opportunities, exacerbated by the restricted range of available services relative to more favoured areas, is all too obvious in the population structure when the results of recent censuses are examined. 'Counterdrift' was the HIDB's early concentrated effort to stem the tide of depopulation and counter the population decline in the Highlands and Islands.

The bilingual policy in Skye is perhaps best expressed in its road signs.

It may seem paradoxical in this age of improved communication, when satellites beam images from the ends of the earth nightly into living rooms, that crofting communities which used to be united by the sea are now divided by it, or at least have to thole long road detours to meet with their neighbours or attend school. The world may have become the global village, but in practical terms there is still a high price to be paid for remoteness at home, a price expressed in terms of the cost of living and travel which affects so much of the crofting province.

Highlands and Islands Enterprise, and in its previous incarnation the Highlands and Islands Development Board, have sought to tackle the geographical disadvantage of location and the economic disadvantage of smallness of scale. The Regional Development Scheme for Skye and the North-west Mainland and the Rural Development Programme have encouraged such things as cooperative endeavour and efficient marketing to draw crofting back from the brink of economic non-viability. The establishment of crofter cooperatives has been actively promoted, with some significant successes.

Diversification is also being actively encouraged, but at the launch of the Rural Development Programme in 1991, an official of the Crofters' Union expressed some reservations over the programme's likely appeal 'to the indigenous hard-working crofter'. In recent times there has been no shortage of non-indigenous crofters waiting in the wings, some with the strength of capital behind them to take advantage of such schemes.

One notable reversal of the depopulation trend has been the resettlement of the Wester Ross township of Scoraig by incomers from a variety of backgrounds, bringing with them a range of skills, such as that of clinker boat building. Their example has demonstrated what an articulate group of individuals can achieve when collectively pressing their case, for they persuaded the local education authority to provide secondary schooling for their older children rather than have them stay in accommodation at Ullapool and attend the high school there.

Just as in Ireland, where the native language maintains its last stronghold in the west, so the crofting communities of the western Highlands and the Hebrides are the heartland of the Gaelic language. Yet even within the Gaidhealtacht the last published census figures revealed that only a fifth of the population aged three and over, amounting to 46,578 people, still used the language in what may be regarded as the indigenous Gaelic areas. The heaviest concentration of Gaelic speakers was in Skye and Lochalsh where 5,166 people (54.2% of the local population) used the language.

A report on language, community and development published by the HIDB noted that 'Few institutions, with the notable exception of the church and some less formal bodies like grazings committees, used Gaelic. . . . The message was clear; Gaelic and development did not go hand in hand'. Efforts have been made of late to extend the provision of bilingual education at primary school level. More visible evidence of bilingual policy is provided by the signs on public buildings and along roads in places like Skye.

Perhaps the most welcome population trend within the crofting area in recent years has been the increasing tendency for younger folk to stay on rather than migrate towards the urban south as was the case for so long. To an extent this is the result of changed economic circumstances generally. For

Crofting communities remain custodians of the living Gaelic language.

example, the recruitment of young men from crofting communities to serve in the merchant navy has dwindled as fleets and maritime labour forces have diminished. At one time this provided an important cash injection into fragile crofting economies. As employment prospects have diminished elsewhere, the pull of other areas has declined. At the same time, in an age that sets increasing store by the quality of life, there has been a growing awareness of the advantages of bringing up a family in a largely unspoiled rural environment, providing that it is economically feasible to do so. Since full-time crofting is unlikely to be viable in the vast majority of circumstances, the need for as wide a range of supplementary occupations as possible is evident.

In this regard, the traditional part-time occupations in inshore fishing and services such as local authority roadwork remain important. From time to time, magazines pick on the more unusual combinations of occupation, but the fact is that crofters must make the most of their local circumstances, so that multiple supplementary incomes are hardly surprising. The traditional

Fishing boats in the harbour at Port of Ness, Lewis. Land and sea have together been the support of communities around Europe's outer edge.

home industries of the islands, Harris tweed and Shetland knitwear, continue to provide a supplement in crofting households, but both have suffered from the whims of changing fashions far away from the island producers.

The weaving of Harris tweed has long provided a second income throughout Lewis and Harris. It is a distinctive and high-quality cloth produced on foot-powered looms, often in a small shed on the croft. The exclusive orb trade mark of the island producers is known the world over as a symbol of quality and individuality. Unfortunately, recent times have seen a worrying drop in demand for tweeds, but the industry has been determined not to stagnate. Recent developments have included experiments with new equipment which would allow the weaving of more versatile double-width tweeds while still employing foot power to work the looms.

Shetland knitwear also has an enviable reputation for high quality. The distinctive 'Fair Isle' patterns have a Scandinavian origin, despite traditions that they came from the fleeing Spanish Armada. Hand-knitting of garments or yokes for machine-knit

Oat stooks beside an island byre with rounded kiln. In many areas the neatly patterned lines of stooks have disappeared as cultivation of the land has declined.

jumpers and cardigans requires deft use of needles, such that generations of crofter wives found this an occupation ideally suited to winter evenings by the fireside. Over the years, the contribution made by Shetland women to crofting incomes has been a significant one.

The coming of the oil industry to Shetland in the form of the giant North Sea oil terminal at Sullom Voe had a major impact on the Shetland economy generally, providing many jobs during the expansionary phase. The income generated from oil-related developments has been a major factor in the provision of improved rural services within Shetland, an obvious benefit to its crofting communities. The impact of the smaller-scale development on the Orkney island of Flotta was less marked, but nevertheless significant in employment terms.

The oil rig construction industry is strongly localised in the inner Moray Firth area, though the Nigg yard in Easter Ross draws its workforce from a wide catchment. The now closed yard at Kishorn in Wester Ross was a significant employer of local labour in its heyday in the late 1970s, bringing many jobs into an area where the primary occupations of crofting, fishing and forestry provided only a restricted employment base. The fabrication yard at Arnish Point outside Stornoway has brought similar employment opportunities to Lewis, though it has known the short-term 'boom and bust' conditions all too familiar in this highly-competitive industry. Nevertheless, in an area with such limited opportunity for supplementing croft incomes, this development has assumed enormous importance, and news of fresh contracts is eagerly awaited throughout the island community.

Small-scale fishing has been a successful supplement to working the land from the earliest days of crofting, and among the crofters' earliest forebears. Inshore fishing for lobsters and other shellfish remains an integral part of many incomes, but constant concern is expressed at the impact of larger, east-coast boats on local stocks, particularly of species like prawns. Crofter-fishermen argue that history shows that their scale of operation is entirely compatible with maintaining the resource, but that the large-scale outside operations are not.

Until recent times, crofters in the Western Isles have maintained the connection with the seaweed resources that were once so important in the days of the kelp industry. Weed has been harvested for processing into alginates, but the industry has also been beset by difficulties which have resulted in closure of local plants, resulting in fluctuating fortunes for the industry at a local level.

Increasingly, attention has been focused on the inshore waters in quite a different way, as sea lochs along the west coast and round the islands have been developed for fish-farming enterprises. With the value of production of farmed salmon now outstripping that of all other livestock production in the Highlands and Islands, the industry has assumed a high profile in development terms. Many younger crofters have the advantage of sea-based, supplementary employment on their doorsteps, in which they can use traditional island skills in an activity which carries fewer physical and economic risks than fishing. Even so, there have been problems associated with oversupply of the European market, for it is an activity that meets stiff competition from producers in a similar setting and circumstance in western Norway. The impact of chemicals used in the industry has been a much-aired source of concern in ecological terms. Despite such problems, however, the value of the industry in terms of local employment and support of local infrastructure would be disputed by very few. For many crofters, work on a fish farm maintains that dual dependence on land and sea which, for so long, has been an important feature of communities along Europe's Atlantic edge.

CHAPTER 13

Crofting towards 2000

As the century draws to a close, what does the future hold for crofting?

It is a question that is easier to ask than to answer. The only certainty is that all shades of opinion will be expressed on the matter, for there are few topics like crofting for stirring up a lively debate. At one extreme there is that fatalism for the future expressed by some of the older members of the crofting community. At the other there is an enthusiasm among younger and progressive crofters, who would like to see a role for themselves and their growing families in an environment in which they would like to stay, provided the formula for the future is a viable one. The contrast between such a positive outlook on the part of younger members of the community who desire to remain within the crofting province and the negative and pessimistic perception so prevalent a decade or two ago could hardly be more marked.

In recent times, crofting has enjoyed an enhanced profile within Scotland as many issues relating to it have received media attention. The debate over the merits of forming crofting trusts to take over the running of existing Department of Agriculture lands, for example, has been a recent example. There have also been the various announcements of incentives offered through the development schemes which have encouraged crofters to improve the viability of their enterprises.

Evidence of change can be seen throughout the crofting area. Livestock housing of an improved and enlarged type is one of the most obvious expressions of this investment, resulting in a cut in the time and effort required for stock management. As a consequence of the reduction in man hours necessary to attend stock, there may, for example, be greater opportunity for a young crofter to seek supplementary work outside, thus adding to the family income. In the improved conditions, cattle can be retained longer before selling, with a resulting increase in value for higher weight or quality. Savings can also be achieved by

The EEC has recognised the special problems of its peripheral areas in awarding funds for infrastructure improvement.

wintering sheep on the croft, instead of sending them outwith the area at the back end of the year as has been the practice for generations due to inadequate local fodder provision.

The push towards increased viability of crofting agriculture has also had an effect on the landscape, resulting in a noticeable 'greening' of areas of previously low-quality grazing. With fodder at the heart of any livestock-producing economy, great emphasis has been laid on the effective production of grass and winter feed. New fencing of pastures, coupled with drainage schemes, have been used to prepare for re-seeding programmes to raise grass quality. Clearly, any move towards improvements in the viability of crofting agriculture must be on a broad front.

In the crofting province as a whole, it is a fact that traditional, community-based effort has often been replaced by an individually-used technology. As a result, that cooperative effort which was once the hallmark of the crofting scene has tended to decline. Yet a strong argument can be advanced for it today in an age of soaring capital costs, and the Highlands and Islands

Development Board were assiduous in encouraging cooperatives.

Post buses, often based on an estate car or even an ordinary saloon, and offering a few seats for passengers, are an established feature of life for scattered communities. Travelling vans, providing services ranging from the banking of money to the supply of butcher meat, also continue to be a part of the crofting scene. For communities with a significant proportion of elderly people who lack the mobility to travel to local service centres, they are an important part of living, yet the economics of keeping a mobile shop on the road threatens the future of many of these important rural services.

Crofting communities have long depended on services supplied from far outwith the area. Even at the beginning of the century, shop boats from Orkney supplied coastal and island communities in the north and west with a range of goods not available locally. For generations, mail order catalogues have provided crofter homes with just about every item of clothing and household goods imaginable, from long johns to curtain lengths. But the increasing trend towards centralisation in the economic geography of the country as a whole has clearly worked against the interests of the more peripheral areas, restricting the range of services available and adding to the cost of living. In national terms the crofting province is clearly the most peripheral of all. On a lighter note, however, it should not be forgotten that in a Hebridean or Shetland crofter's perception of geographical location, the south-east of England might be regarded as decidedly remote and peripheral when viewed from an island perspective! As freight charges rise, basic costs increase in relation to those borne by the population in less remote situations, so that cost-cutting must permanently exercise the minds of crofters determined to make a reasonable family living.

By contrast with the difficulties of geographical remoteness, modern high technology is constrained by no such problems. The business section of a national newspaper recently profiled a Sutherland crofter of a new type: one who runs both a flock of sheep and an international consultancy from her home, aided by the latest in telecommunications equipment.

Younger, progressive crofters received an unexpected accolade from Scottish Office Minister, Lord Sanderson, speaking in

Modern agricultural buildings express the impact of recent development schemes on the Isle of Skye.

Inverness in the summer of 1990. His description of them as 'Mrs Thatcher's boys', was quickly parodied in a cartoon in the *West Highland Free Press*, showing an older crofter impassively viewing a passing tractor driven by a 'yuppie' character in smart pinstripe suit with Filofax sticking out of his back pocket.

Diversification has become something of a keyword for agriculture in Scotland in the last few years as the thorny problem of farm surpluses is addressed. The government has not been slow to point out the advantages nationally of broadening the rural economic base beyond agriculture. In the diversification debate there are those who have pointed to crofting as a model for the future, given that crofters have always had to look to more than their land for an income.

An even greater degree of diversification will be important for many crofters in the future on two counts. First, it is the means of boosting income, and second, it may be the means of offsetting any decline in livestock prices which may occur. The depressed market for beef after the BSE (mad cow disease) hysteria swept the country was a sobering reminder that when it comes to food, constant demand cannot always be relied upon. The slump in livestock prices at the end of the 1980s was a demoralising experience for many younger and progressive crofters who had put effort and finance into raising higher quality livestock than crofts in many areas had produced before. At the same time, less favourable political attitudes towards farm support within the EEC could mean that producers in more peripheral areas become even more hard pressed.

Throughout the Highlands, forestry has become a major alternative use of the land in the latter half of this century. Government has been keen to encourage private investment in tree planting, so here would seem to be a possible alternative to traditional land-use practice. However, there are major problems because of the particular circumstances of crofting. The Crofter Forestry (Scotland) Bill, sponsored by Western Isles MP Calum MacDonald, seeks to end the situation whereby any trees planted by crofting tenants, once grown beyond a certain size, are deemed to be the property of the landlord. When passed, the law would give crofters the legal right to the trees which they had planted. It would also entitle them to the relevant grants which are on offer as an incentive to increased tree planting. Crofting townships could thereby obtain grants through the established mechanism of their grazings committees, thus opening the way to afforestation of suitable areas of common grazing. Forestry plantations already exist outwith crofting land in some of the islands and western mainland areas where crofting is well established, so that afforestation is practicable. As part of a properly managed approach to land use, forestry could therefore play a role in balancing environmental and development interests in suitable parts of the Highlands and Islands.

The place of crofting in the debate over environmental matters is another issue which is increasingly aired. In particular, the suggestion that national parks be designated in areas such as Wester Ross has provoked a fierce debate, with little local enthusiasm for the proposal. When national parks were designated in England and Wales in the post-war years, it was considered unnecessary at the time to give areas of the Scottish countryside such statutory status. Now, with increased leisure

Mobile shops and banks play an important role in servicing outlying crofting communities, many of which have a large proportion of elderly residents.

time and improved accessibility, it is suggested that these areas may suffer from too many trampling feet, and from a lack of planning and development control to maintain their essential quality of wilderness.

At a public meeting held in Lochcarron in June 1990, a speaker asserted that the idea of a national park was not appropriate for Wester Ross where the environment had been exceptionally well maintained for generations by local people. Others feel that control over the management of any national park would be outwith the local community, and would not be sensitive enough to local aspirations. Another argument, based on the experience of some of the southern national parks, is that designation actually attracts more people, resulting in increased pressure on sensitive and sometimes fragile areas.

An important part of the reasoning behind designation of land in upland areas of England and Wales was that they possessed a strong cultural and historical interest as well as high landscape quality. Undoubtedly, crofting contributes a great

deal to the cultural and historical interest of an area like Wester
Ross, but crofters are wary of any constraint which may be
placed upon them by such an official designation of land.
Crofting cannot exist for the benefit of tourists, the local
argument runs, but must be free to evolve and develop in a way
that ensures its economic viability.

It has been suggested that a more sympathetic solution to the
problem of how best to care for the environment in Wester Ross
would be to designate more Environmentally Sensitive Areas
such as exist in the outer isles. These would allow support for
continuing agricultural practices which have maintained the
landscape and the environment as it is today. Certainly, it could
be strongly argued that the high natural interest of the machair
lands of the Outer Hebrides is directly related to the way in
which it has been managed over many generations. Crofter and
corncrake have survived in a sort of symbiosis that has allowed
the latter to persist in the islands when intensive land
management have driven it out of mainland areas.

At a conference held in Skye in 1990, organised jointly by
Comunn na Gaidhlig and Sabhal Mor Ostaig, the local Gaelic
college, suggestions were put forward by Dr James Hunter for
designating the north-west of Scotland a European Heritage
Area. The concept of sustainability was advanced, in which
development is not put before the cost to the natural
environment. Previously, increased agricultural output and the
support of less favoured area producers have been regarded as
the obvious recipients of financial aid. But now, at a point in
time when such conventional arguments for support for crofting
seem unlikely to find much sympathy, it is argued that sustaining
wildlife and habitat, human (often crofter) communities and
the Gaelic language and culture should be encouraged.

The high quality of landscape and of environment generally
in the crofting areas of the Highlands and Islands is a major
resource which tourism has only partly exploited. In fact, the
tourist industry has long contributed to the diversification of
the crofting economy, but recent times have seen a significant
and continuing interest in tourist-related development, with
the provision of self-catering and other on-croft facilities. In an
increasingly 'green' and environmentally-sensitive age, there

Fish farming has added a new dimension to both landscape and way of life in many crofting areas. Salmon farm, Wester Ross.

must be a potential for growth in a setting of such visual impact and scenic and cultural attraction.

Sustainable tourism is the desirable aim, one that would bring a living to many within crofting communities without destroying their essential character. Whatever the value of scenery, the historical and cultural attraction, the recreation potential and the peace and quiet, the fact is that without the availability of the local infrastructure and services the real potential for tourist development in the crofting province would not be realised. Through the provision of bed-and-breakfast facilities at croft houses, the letting of purpose-built self-catering chalets, and paid employment in tourist-related activities, the tourist industry is a significant adjunct to crofting in many places.

An interesting development has been the introduction of Crofting Life Holidays, a diversification initiative launched by the Highlands and Islands Development Board. Potential visitors are invited to sample the attractions of living for a few days in a township with a crofting family. Many of the participating crofters on the west are Gaelic-speaking, allowing visitors an opportunity to acquire some conversational Gaelic as well. If they wish to become practically involved (something which may have an increasing appeal for desk-bound professionals), guests are also able to take part in seasonal croft work, such as haymaking or peat-cutting — an ideal antidote to the stresses of urban living! Indeed, there is a royal precedent for this, as the Prince of Wales spent a few days in the Western Isles some years ago, helping with the manual work on a croft.

Ironically, the unspoiled nature of the environment, which attracts so many people to visit crofting areas, has raised its own problems in recent times, as designations of Sites of Special Scientific Interest by the Nature Conservancy Council have increased. Recently, a Strath Halladale crofter accused the Council of presiding over a modern version of the Highland Clearances. The accusation centred over the need to provide an environmental assessment for an area which was to be the subject of a development plan by the local crofter grazings committee for reseeding and shelter-belt planting. Unfortunately, conservation has often been perceived in the north as being associated with a distant bureaucracy. In a part of the world where the memory of outside, southern, interference is still very strong, it is perhaps not hard to seek an explanation for why such perceptions exist and conflicts of interest flare up.

By contrast with the outward migration of the younger members of families that so characterised the crofting area well into the post-war era, many townships have recently seen a trend towards a middle-class uptake of vacant crofts. With prices pushed beyond the reach of young crofters setting out in life, the social fabric and outlook of crofting townships would seem to be in for a change.

At a time when the European dimension is being discussed in relation to so many aspects of our life and society, it is not surprising that the issue of crofting in a wider context should be increasingly aired. One of the problems, of course, is precisely that crofting has been perceived largely as a form of agriculture teetering on the edge of viability, when it is clearly much more a way of life based on the land, only in a minority of cases

For many communities, sheep have become the mainstay of the crofting way of life.

deriving its total support from it. The situation is emphasised in, for example, the involvement of the Department of Agriculture in the matter of crofter housing. In this age of continental awareness, there has been a tendency to compare crofting with farming systems in Europe. But such comparison inevitably shows it up in a bad light as a form of land-working that at best is far removed from the large and productive lowland units, and at worst is a peripheral anachronism.

The huge cereal-producing units of lowland England and the Paris basin, which have helped create the great farm surpluses of modern times, are recent developments which have pushed productivity of the land to its limits. In so doing they have also resulted in a catalogue of environmental catastrophes such as soil erosion, pollution of ground water, and a serious reduction in wildlife habitat and scenic quality.

The part-time, family-run unit is by no means a feature only of Europe's outermost edge. My family and I recently spent a farmhouse holiday in Jutland where the income of the small farm was generated by the farmer's job at a local sawmill and his wife's summer earnings in their tourist-related enterprise, as well as from livestock sales off the farm. The reality is that this style of part-time farming and multiple job-holding is far from being unique. It is still a strong feature of farming throughout western Europe, and one which has survived the trends of large-scale mechanisation, decline in rural population and increase in farm size. On the same small Danish farm, the planting of broad shelter belts of mixed species had not only added to the scenic interest of the area, but also provided a habitat for birds and other wildlife. Significantly, it also contributed to the farm income, through fees paid for shooting rights for game such as roe deer.

Crofting enjoys positive advantages when it comes to diversification and multiple job-holding. Even as a tenant, a crofter faces no impediment to using the croft land for subsidiary occupations that will generate income. He or she also has the right to put up any buildings that may be required to house some ancillary business, whether to provide chalet accommodation for tourists or to build a shed for some craft industry. In statutory terms, crofting enjoys the benefit of the rights so vigorously fought for last century. In the 21st century, there is a potential in those rights for extending further the diversification which has always been a feature of crofting, but which is now hailed as such a desirable approach to land use and holding.

Paradoxically for those who perceive crofting to be some sort of hopelessly outmoded farming system, the lowland agricultural areas of Britain which were affected by the greatest drive towards farm enlargement and increased biochemical and mechanical technology are precisely those which have been drained of their people. Rural villages may be seeing an increase in population, but it is not a land-based people who are moving in to the renovated cottages once occupied by farm workers. Yet in many crofting districts, despite the rural depopulation of the past, people are still on the land in significant numbers. There could hardly be a greater contrast than that between the sparsely-peopled prairie farmscape of Lincolnshire and the well-populated croft lands of the northern parts of Lewis or of Tiree. The modern or modernised house in the rural villages of lowland England are just as likely to be occupied by commuters from

Old ways continue to survive, as in this North Sutherland township, where the crofter prepares to sow his oat crop by hand. April 1991.

urban areas. But their country living really means a countryside abode. In Lewis it has a wider meaning, for there the modern and modernised houses are occupied by crofters whose roots are firmly in their croftlands, though they have a multiplicity of ancillary occupations for their support.

As long as economic viability was equated with moving on to bigger and better things, especially in terms of size of landholdings, it is perhaps hardly surprising that crofting was regarded as some kind of fossilised form of agricultural system entirely lacking in a future. It has been pointed out several times that The Napier Commission in the 1880s, the Congested Districts Board in the 1890s and the Crofters Commission of 1960 were much concerned with the notion that size of landholding was the ultimate factor on which viability depended. But socio-economic factors have changed, and what might have been viewed as an economically viable landholding even a decade or two ago might be regarded now as inadequate for a family living.

The land is of prime importance to crofting and always will be, whatever degree of diversification occurs. That effective use of the land has been in retreat is, however, all too sadly obvious throughout the crofting province where the once-cultivated inbye land of many crofts consists now only of sheep grazing. This is not to argue for a return to the well-worked cultivation rigs of the past, patterned by stooked oats and neatly stacked hay, and so evocatively captured in the many black and white photographs of a departed age. These scenes from the past are an expression of a style of living that is not appropriate to the present, a living that was determined by the need to be as self-sufficient as possible. Yet if the land will always be at the very heart of crofting, as a Wester Ross crofter so strongly asserted to me recently, then it can be argued that it should be concerned with making as significant a contribution as possible in agricultural terms. To this end, the development and incentive schemes of recent times have an important role to play.

Despite improvements in the communications network, geography will always impose its own problems upon crofting communities. While a bridge to Skye may make that particular island more attractive still to would-be aspirants to the crofting way of life, there will undoubtedly be other islands where the problems of location will compound the difficulties of maintaining a viable living and population. In such circumstances it may then become necessary positively to encourage incomers to settle, as happened recently on the Shetland island of Fetlar. Advertisements placed in national magazines have been resorted to in an effort to boost the population total of just over 80, predominantly crofters, and many of them elderly. Paradoxically, Fetlar was the scene of some of the Shetland evictions last century. In economic terms, marginality is the twin of peripherality. Outside economic forces, over which crofters have no control, may prove nothing short of disastrous for already fragile communities. At the depressed 1990 livestock sales in Shetland, the *Press & Journal* reported that only four Fetlar crofters succeeded in selling their sheep.

Significantly, it has recently been suggested that new crofts, or something resembling crofts, might be created in more favoured parts of the country, well outwith the present crofting province. Their advocates would see in them a way of maintaining a viable rural population and ensuring the survival of social services such as schools and other aspects of the infrastructure which rural depopulation inevitably threatens.

While anchored to the land over which their ancestors fought so vigorously last century, crofters are nevertheless being called upon to respond to changing situations and opportunities. That they are capable of rising to a challenge has been demonstrated many times in the past. As a new millennium develops, this living at the edge, which has challenged human determination since earliest times, is doubtless set to continue.

Further Reading

Bardgett, F. *North Coast Parish: Strathy and Halladale*, 1990

Cameron, A. D. *Go Listen to the Crofters*, Acair 1986 (A fascinating account of the Napier Commission)

Devine, T. M. *The Great Highland Famine*, John Donald 1988

Donaldson, G. *The Scots Overseas*, Robert Hale 1966

Dunlop, J. *The British Fisheries Society 1786-1893*, John Donald 1978

Fenton, A. *The Northern Isles: Orkney and Shetland*, John Donald 1978 (The best account of the ethnography of the Northern Isles)

Fenton, A. *The Island Blackhouse*, HMSO 1978

Geikie, Sir A. *Scottish Reminiscences*, James Maclehose 1906

Grant, I. *Highland Folkways*, Routledge & Kegan Paul 1961

Knox, S. *The Making of the Shetland Landscape*, John Donald 1985

MacArthur, E. M. *Iona. The Living memory of a Crofting Community*, Edinburgh University Press 1990

MacDonald, J. M. *Highland Ponies*, Eneas Mackay 1937

MacLean, M. and Carrell, C. *As an Fhearann. From the Land*, Mainstream 1986

MacPhail, I. M. M. *The Crofters' War*, Acair 1989 (A first-class account of the many events of the period)

Mitchell, A. *The Past in the Present*, David Douglas 1880

Richards, E. *A History of the Highland Clearances* (2 Vols.), Croom Helm 1982, 1985

Salaman, R. *The History and Social Influence of the Potato*, Cambridge University Press 1985

Somers, R. *Letters from the Highlands on the Famine of 1846*, Melven Press 1985

Scottish Vernacular Buildings Working Group, *Highland Vernacular Building*, SVBWG 1989

Scottish Vernacular Buildings Working Group, *North Sutherland Studies*, SVBWG 1987

Thompson, F. *Crofting Years*, Luath Press 1984

Willis, D. P. *Moorland and Shore: Their Place in the Human Geography of Old Orkney*, Department of Geography, University of Aberdeen 1983

Willis, D. P. *Sand and Silence. Lost Villages of the North*, University of Aberdeen Centre for Northern Studies, 1986

The *West Highland Free Press*, published weekly at Broadford in Skye, frequently carries articles and comment on crofting matters.

The *Scottish Geographical Magazine*, Vol. 103, No. 2, September 1987 contains an interesting set of articles on crofting, marking the centenary of the first Crofting Act. These include:
J. B. Caird *The Creation of Crofts and New Settlement Patterns in the Highlands and Islands of Scotland*
C. W. J. Withers *Highland-Lowland Migration and the Making of the Crofting Community, 1755-1891*
D. E. Meek *'The Land Question Answered from the Bible': The Land Issue and the Development of a Highland Theology of Liberation*
D. J. MacCuish *Crofting Legislation Since 1886*
J. Shaw Grant *Government Agencies and the Highlands since 1945*
J. M. Bryden *Crofting in the European Context*

Dr James Hunter has produced many interesting articles and commentaries on crofting matters in recent times. His book *The Making of the Crofting Community* (John Donald 1976) remains a classic in crofting literature.

The Crofters Commission's own publications are a most valuable source of information. They include the *Annual Reports*, the *Guide to the Crofting Acts*, and *Crofting in the '90s*, a strategy statement by the Commission, published May, 1991.

Index